"*The Micro-Script Rules* is dead on—it's how to verbalize a point of difference. And without a one, you better have a low price."

—JACK TROUT, CO-AUTHOR OF THE LEGENDARY
POSITIONING: THE BATTLE FOR YOUR MIND AND REPOSITIONING:
MARKETING IN AN ERA OF COMPETITION, CHANGE, AND CRISIS

"The missing ingredient in most marketing is memorability. Bill Schley has developed a list of Micro-Script rules that solve that problem. Well-organized and well-written."

—AL RIES, CO-AUTHOR OF THE LEGENDARY POSITIONING:
THE BATTLE FOR YOUR MIND AND WAR IN THE BOARDROOM

"Bill Schley's insights and examples are invaluable to anyone selling a political candidate or a new tax law, an established brand or a new product."

—DAN GOODGAME, FORMER WASHINGTON BUREAU CHIEF FOR
TIME MAGAZINE, COMMUNICATIONS CONSULTANT

"This ground-breaking book spells out the power of Micro-Scripts and enables readers to create and utilize them in any situation that calls for persuasive communication."

—KEN LLOYD, PH.D., BESTSELLING CO-AUTHOR
(WITH DR. DONALD MOINE), UNLIMITED SELLING POWER

"Google indexes over 1.5 *Trillion* URL's. 300 billion messages bombard us—per second. It's a global pandemic of message madness. Most are loaded with self-serving corporate gobbledygook that delivers zero value. Too much info. Too many words.

Bill Schley's *The Micro-Script Rules* shows you how to put meaning into your message and get it past the madness. To quote one of history's greatest thinkers, "A child of five could understand this—quick, someone fetch a child of five" —Groucho Marx. *The Micro-Script Rules*—quick, fetch it."

—STEVE KAYSER, EDITOR, CINCOM EXPERT ACCESS,
THE ONLINE BUSINESS MAGAZINE

"If positioning is the battle for your mind, Micro-Scripts are the weapons that win the battle for your brand. In *The Micro-Script Rules*, Bill Schley has made it possible for any business to create a word of mouth message. Read this book and you will have your customers happily repeating your Dominant Selling Idea."

—JAY EHRET, CEO AND FOUNDER, WWW.THEMARKETINGSPOT.COM

"Bill Schley's *The Micro-Script Rules* is the best book I've read on how to boil down a complex message into a few memorable words that an audience would remember and want to spread."

—MARK LEVY, FOUNDER OF LEVY INNOVATION, AUTHOR OF *ACCIDENTAL GENIUS: USING WRITING TO GENERATE YOUR BEST IDEAS, INSIGHT, AND CONTENT*

"I find myself recommending Microscripts to people in so many different fields: teachers, entrepreneurs, lawyers. Why? Because this is how the brain works. It is so simple, yet so fundamental. Through this witty, creative little treasure, Bill has captured the essence of how we think."

—DONNA M. VOLPITTA, ED.D.

"*The Micro-Script Rules* should be required reading for every candidate and campaign consultant. Political candidates and pundits **talk** about the importance of *a campaign message*, but rarely understand what that means. Bill Schley's work is the simple explanation."

—JIM KITCHENS, PH. D., PRESIDENT OF THE KITCHENS GROUP

"WOW, one of the most important books you will read in your lifetime!"

—JASON JENNINGS, BESTSELLING AUTHOR, *LESS IS MORE, THINK BIG–ACT SMALL* AND *HIT THE GROUND RUNNING*

"As Bill Schley shows with compelling examples of success, Micro-Scripts are big marketing. In the old days scale and media buying power won. In today's always-on, YouTube and Twitter-centric world, anybody can dominate a market with a few well-placed words. Especially you. So what are you waiting for?"

—DAVID MEERMAN SCOTT, BESTSELLING AUTHOR OF *THE NEW RULES OF MARKETING & PR* AND CO-AUTHOR OF *MARKETING LESSONS FROM THE GRATEFUL DEAD*

The Micro-Script Rules

It's not what people hear.
It's what they repeat…

Bill Schley

To Annie
the original masterpiece

WidenerBooks

N.W. Widener, Inc., New York
1105 Lexington Avenue, Suite 300
New York, NY 10075
www.widenerbooks.com

First Published in 2010 by N.W. Widener, Inc., New York

10 9 8 7 6 5 4 3 2 1

PUBLISHER'S NOTE: This publication is designed to provide accurate and authoritative information in regard to the subject matter covered. It is sold with the understanding that the publisher is not engaged in rendering legal, accounting or other professional services. Any brand names or individual names are used in an editorial fashion. If you require legal advice or other expert assistance, you should seek the services of a competent professional.

Publisher's Cataloging-in-Publication

    Schley, Bill.
      The micro-script rules : it's not what people hear,
    it's what they repeat— / Bill Schley.
      p. cm.
      Includes bibliographical references and index.
      ISBN-13: 978-0-9826941-0-7
      ISBN-10: 0-9826941-0-5
      ISBN-13: 978-0-9826941-1-4
      ISBN-10: 0-9826941-1-3
      [etc.]

      1. Branding (Marketing) 2. Communication.
    I. Title.

HF5415.1255.S35 2010   658.8'27
                     QBI10-600104

Printed in the United States of America • Designed by Paul Lussier

Contents

Contents

Contents

The Secret Email

I got a secret forwarded email at the start of the Great Recession, right after the collapse of Bear Stearns, AIG and Lehman. It was designed to scare the bejeezus out of me and the 97 million others they knew would see it—the notes from an emergency meeting of all 100 CEOs at Sequoia Capital, the legendary Silicon Valley venture capital firm:

> Forget about getting ahead, we're talking survive. All assumptions prior to today are wrong. Do it right and you may be able to capitalize on this downturn and live...*Nail your marketing message, now.* Measure everything and cut what's not working.

A key takeaway: You can't quit marketing and selling and stay in business. But if you keep spending fantasy bucks and don't deliver an ROI, you're toast.

Needing to advise our marketing clients amidst this mayhem, I started thinking and reading about how humans focus and succeed in times of great stress. It led me to the cognitive science of *heuristics*—the *rules of thumb* that drive our gut feelings, influencing just about everything we do. And after twenty-five years in the persuasion business, it was an epiphany—not just for marketers and brand people but for anyone with a vital message to tell—which is the basis of this unadorned little book.

Herein lies the secret of communicating your ideas with the most simple, penetrating, and yes, viral power—in a world that from now on will demand nothing less.

Part I

The Story,
The Rules

Introduction

"If the glove doesn't fit, you must acquit."

It was a simple rhyming couplet. Yet it vaporized the state's entire, nine-month case. It was all the jury remembered—and fifteen years later, what we remember still. It wasn't just a sound bite. For the defense, it was magic...

It has always been true. From now on, it'll just be *more* true: The right five words will always beat 5,000.

Stories are more important to tell than ever, but you need to know how to tell one in about one line or less.

The new world of media is actually getting much less complicated than the old media, so stop stressing out.

It's more crucial that a brand work one-to-one, from the ground up, than the top down—that is, if you want to *be* a brand, a successful politician, non-profit, teacher or just a great communicator in our new hyper-connected world.

There. For everyone who needs to get back to their Blackberries, that's pretty much the whole book.

But for those of you who want to know how to do this for yourself—how to transform an idea so it penetrates like a silver bullet; who want the human secret ALL great communicators have understood and wielded since biblical times—we've conveniently attached the remaining 170 pages of this little primer.

You get there by following what we call the *Micro-Script Rules*, whether you're a global corporation, a presidential candidate or a golf shop. Believe me, they are disarmingly short and simple. It's 170 pages because we used a lot of examples.

So let's begin. Once you get how it works and why it will change the way you offer your ideas to the world from now on, you'll be glad you read.

"Look At That Giant Wave, Heading for Our Hotel."

Isn't it interesting and a little ironic that when an organism is mortally threatened, when the gun is pointing at your nose, when the tornado is coming up your driveway, or the plane's on fire and there's a parachute and a door, things *finally* start to get…simple.

It works at every level of the food chain, all the way down to cells and organs. When the body thinks it's freezing, for example, it shifts to *the heart of the matter*, literally. It shuts down blood flow to the extremities and directs it all to your heart and your brain. You're prioritizing big time. It doesn't have to be told. It doesn't have commitment issues. It's truth time. It's simple time. And above all, it's hyper-effectiveness time.

Heuristics—Our Rules of Thumb

Behavioral scientists tell us that in moments of crisis or uncertainty, we shift to intuition that is remarkably fast and accurate—unconscious intelligence that skips normal reasoning because it doesn't have time. Our intuition comes from a built-in set of *heuristics*, more commonly known as *rules of thumb*—which are just simple mental instructions to take preset actions for a best-chance outcome. We're born with them. They tell us how to make snap judgments—act instantly on inconclusive data—without analyzing a whole set of facts.

But what they're really showing us is the heart of the matter—the true bottom line—not just faster but often better than process-laden analytics—by telling us to do the opposite of what our schools and corporations have taught us from day one: they make us *discard* information, not collect more of it—to get smarter.

This is really important so I'll say it again:

When things get complicated and tense, built-in heuristics or rules of thumb direct us to a much smaller set of more vital data to deliver us to the heart of the matter. They tell us that *simpler makes us smarter*. Data overload gums up the works. Too much information makes us dumber.

The Lawyer Got It Right

Our brains know this, even when experts don't. After eons of evolution, our brains are wired to simplify, they like to simplify—and they find it irresistible when others help us simplify.

Johnny Cochran, OJ Simpson's lawyer, understood this when he offered his famous eight-word solution to the jury in exchange for nine months of testimony, and asked them to choose. He said, you can take a billion bits of evidence, or save the trouble and just remember one thing: OJ was framed by racist cops.

And then he offered them a little script to make remembering easy—something we call a **Micro-Script:** *If the glove doesn't fit you must acquit.* A mini-logic set, in a memorable little word package, that could be repeated by everyone.

Ten years before the age of social networks and universal texting, Johnny Cochran knew the power of turning 8,000 words into eight. He knew about Micro-Scripts.

Today, when your message needs to fit on a cell phone screen, a Twitter post or the back of a T-shirt, and is competing with a zillion other conversations from every conceivable direction, that would be pretty important, wouldn't you think? Well, hold that thought.

Ever Caught a Ball?

Our built-in heuristics are ancient and they help us in big and little ways. Like when your caveman buddy throws a rock at your head, they tell you when to duck. According to Professor Gerd Gigerenzer, you use what's called the Gaze Heuristic, a shortcut that evolved over millions of years for animals to intercept moving prey. It saves the brain from running a thousand differential math equations to calculate the trajectory. Your brain gives you one, practical, rule of thumb instead:

Fix your gaze on the rock. If the <u>angle stays constant</u>, duck!

That's it. One decision to make, one button to push that automatically triggers a whole set of actions in the right order. It's the same rule of thumb a dog uses to catch a Frisbee or an outfielder uses to snag a pop fly.[1]

All Heuristics All the Time...

But our rules are no longer just for times of stress. We make a constant stream of bets to fill in the blanks as we go about our normal day. We calculate the value of everything we see, every second[2]—from the items we pluck off the supermarket shelf to our route home in traffic. Unconscious rules of thumb cause our gut feelings, which have three things in common: 1) they appear quickly, 2) for reasons we are generally not aware, and 3) they're strong enough for us to act on the least possible information.[3]

Again, we like to work this way. After a zillion years, the brain naturally defaults to "fast and frugal."[4] And for all of us who would presume to communicate with other humans amid the unprecedented economic, social and media chaos zipping all around us—the hyper-connected world—respecting this default is no longer optional. It's time to get with the program.

What If We Could Bottle This?

What if we found the rules of thumb for communicating ideas that were so simple and powerful, we could capture the kind of focus we reach at times of stress, and turn it into branding that was suddenly sharp and differentiating, or presentations that people could remember and repeat ten minutes or ten days after you left the room? Or a political speech that set the voters in motion? Or tantalizing Tweets or great Google Abstracts? Or lessons for our sixth grade class? Or any kind of message we wanted to succeed in any of the new media? And what if a big, unintended consequence was they made our marketing intuition and strategy better too, especially in branding—because we couldn't even think about applying these rules without keeping our focus—they made clarity the default?

Well, we have found them—as you're about find out.

If what I'm describing sounds familiar, it's not just that it's somewhat intuitive. Unconscious intelligence has indeed been popularized lately, most notably by Malcolm Gladwell in *Blink*, his book about "thinking without thinking." Gladwell's premise came largely from the academic writings and research of cognitive psychologists like Gerd Gigerenzer, Timothy Wilson, Gary Klein—and by extension the Nobel laureate Herbert A. Simon, and George Polya who wrote about heuristic problem solving all the way back in 1945. So the notion of unconscious intelligence is not new.

This book uses these learnings to ask a different question in this hyper-connected age: *What if we could apply it to human communication?*

Rules of Thumb for the Great Communicator

This book is about revealing those few heuristics that will set you up for the most penetrating communication you've ever had—simply by working the way our brains want to work. It will affect the way you brand, the way you pitch, the way you conduct a political campaign—the way you try to persuade anyone from now on.

Some are as fundamental as the ancient, unconscious ones I mentioned above.

But other rules we can invent to perform specific tasks—once we know how these things work. We've learned to make up heuristics throughout human history to deal with anything dangerous, challenging, complex, or uncertain—from sports to spelling to safety. *(Where there's smoke there's fire).*

Please note that from here on: The words *heuristics* and *rules of thumb* are synonymous and can be used interchangeably.[5]

You'll see that all of them will have a few things in common. They are:

1. Simple

2. High yield—automatically set up the right actions with one decision

3. Few in number

4. Require minimal information to be triggered

And critically, when we decide to invent them, they must be—

5. Say-able in words—repeatable words

The Rules Promise

With these Rules you will:

- **Discard distractions and useless data to get directly to the heart of the matter—*and stay there.***
- **Find your creative solutions quicker.**
- **Actually boost your intuition, sharpen your strategy.**
- **Create communications that work the way the brain likes to work.**

They will improve your results in the new media world, the old world...or any world.

CHAPTER 1

The Four Big Rules

The Problem's Not Apathy, It's Entropy

Great communicating or any great achievement in business is directly proportional to our capacity for cutting through the crap, finding the heart of the matter, making it our strategy, and then staying there. Ask any successful doctor, lawyer, investor, financial professional, entrepreneur or inventor. You find the heart, hold on to it through thick and thin, then spend the rest of your time connecting the dots. The more complicated the world gets, the more important the heart becomes.

It sounds simple and it is simple. We all know the conventional wisdom. "K.I.S.S." we all say. Stay on message. Couldn't be easier.

Except—for some insane reason, when it comes to communication. When it comes to making clear, consistent messages about our brands, our candidates or even the products we sell, we're good for about a minute. Then we invariably get distracted, veer off the road and drive our strategy into the ditch. Trust us. We've been watching this happen at the best companies in the world for more than twenty-five years. It happens every time, and it happens in seconds unless someone has got a white-knuckled grip on the steering wheel with one hand, while swatting away a constant barrage of "helpful," irrelevant dilutions with the other.

Call it the entropy gene. Entropy is the scientific principle which states that in all of nature, order tends to go to dis-order. In other words, we don't stay focused.

It's the true Achilles heel of would-be great communicators; the single biggest preventer of powerful, cost-efficient messaging—not to mention that mythical great brand. We get distracted by colleagues, by committees, by politics, by points of view, by gimmicks, by research that misses the point, by over-analysis and the proliferating number of new mediums. We can't stay simple. We can't hold the center.

The Cure: *The Micro-Script Rules*

Again, it's the opposite of what big organizations and rational institutions have always taught us. The cure is not to compulsively gather more data until we overload our circuits and short out.

The secret is to identify a go-to set of communication heuristics that let us discard the unnecessary, see the heart of the matter and thus, the answer. These rules must be instantly at our fingertips—just like the ones a race car driver or skydiver has.

All together we will call them the **Micro-Script Rules.** They act as a remarkable focus engine. And if that alone were their contribution to communications, it'd be worth the whole price of admission. Or this book.

We'll begin by introducing you to four real biggies. Master rules that are so all-encompassing, we'll call them…The Four Big Rules.

The rest of the rules of thumb will be more practical and specific—designed to make the Big Rules (BRs) work for you. They're the ones we'll carry around in our heads for regular guidance—in strategic sessions, creative meetings, sales presentations, public speeches, or on the fly.

The Big Four

BR 1:
It's What They Repeat

The first one is so basic, so obvious, I can't believe even *we* missed its significance until the digital age arrived—and we're professionals.

Frank Luntz, the prominent Republican word man who takes credit for teaching the GOP how to use language like *Death-tax* vs. Estate tax and *No child left behind* instead of The Mandatory Punitive School Testing Law in order to shape debates and win elections, propounded this basic principle for effective communicating. Luntz said:

"It's not what you say, it's what people hear."

Sounds good—but it's not bottom-line enough for us to actually create those effective communications. We must go one step deeper to where the rubber meets the road in today's hyper-connected reality.

To communicate your idea in a digitally-powered, consumer-driven, word-of-mouth world, it's not what you tell people or even what they hear that drives communication. In today's world, what's most important is:

What people want to _repeat_, after they've heard you.

I'll repeat: The most important thing is not what people hear, it's what they want to repeat after they've heard you.

This is big. If you've ever been in kindergarten, or sat in a focus group, it will come as no surprise that what you are saying about yourself or your product and what *others* are saying is not guaranteed to be the same thing.

They won't say anything because you tell them to. They say it only if and because they want to say it, they like saying it, they gain from saying it. And for that, they have to understand it, believe it, like it, feel it's valuable to them, be moved by it, remember it, and think it reflects their inherent point of view.

Then, if they do, they will literally say it in two critical places. First, they'll say it to themselves, over and over again in the way they frame and order their own thoughts; and second, they'll say it to their friends, both personal and professional. The words they say to themselves are the words they'll use.

This is where the marketing and selling power is in today's world.

Why?

Because of Big Rule #2...

BR 2:

The Master Medium
Every Screen's A Word of Mouth Machine

In the old days, there were only three mediums: TV, radio and print. Today there's one new master medium that supersedes everything.

(You thought I was going to say hundreds of mediums. But no, it's really one master medium).

And it's not the Internet or social networking. Those are just mechanical. It's a brand new, 50,000-year-old medium.

You know it as **Word of Mouth.**

Now it's worth pausing for a minute to think about how amazing and ironic this is. That in a world creating new forms of electronic media every day—from the Internet to iPhones to social networking communities—marketing gurus are saying that simple Word of Mouth, the most ancient advertising medium of all, is once again the most powerful on the planet! It's the medium that the whole phenomenon of viral networking and marketing runs on. The magic that can turn a tiny fashion fad in New York City or a frumpy singer on *Britain's Got Talent* into a global phenomenon overnight—can literally only happen one way—via Word of Mouth.

The Word of Mouth Machines

In fact, you can quit stressing out about keeping up with the wildly morphing, dizzying new world of media and zillions of new gadgets if you just stop and let yourself realize—all these new personal digital machines like iPhones and Blackberries and social websites are nothing more than twenty-first century, electronic *Word of Mouth Machines*. They give the power to anyone to broadcast their WOM content, not just over the backyard fence, but around the planet to whole related communities in nanoseconds.

The new machines have simply made caveman communications scalable.

But all this still doesn't explain *why* the most ancient medium of all is suddenly the killer app all over again—why so many consumers are drawn back to it now.

Well, first of all, it never went away, it was just interrupted for seven or eight decades by version 1.0 of electronic mass media—radio and TV—which were too primitive to go both ways. They only broadcast one way, company to consumer. Now, two-way technology has simply let us to get back to Word of Mouth.

But the biggest reason is that Word of Mouth takes the most important <u>success</u> factor in communication and flips it on its head. WOM has changed the source and the sequence, for building...

Trust.

You see, with one-way media, the message comes first, then product trial, then if it works, trust follows at the end of a long sequence—a cumulative result.

The problem is that too often, people believed the marketing, and got burned. They felt abused and humiliated. And consumers HATE when that happens. Too many companies over-marketed and under-delivered in the last century, and that's made people cynical.

So people aren't so quick to trust the corporate authorities anymore.

Who do they trust?

They trust other members of their own group—their friends, and their own eyes.

Word of Mouth solves the trust problem by delivering trust right *up front*—a personal endorsement from someone I know and believe at the beginning of the transaction. With WOM—either trust comes first or there won't *be* a relationship. Won't be trial, won't be anything. It reduces the risk. And it doesn't get switched off by the remote.

And just to get philosophical for a second—WOM is so utterly fundamental to human communications, it shouldn't be considered "just a tactic" any more than trust is a tactic. It can't be manipulated any more than trust can be manipulated. Word of Mouth has to be earned as a result of honest, good behavior and real performance. Like trust, achieving it must be a strategic objective for any marketer or communicator.

But that said, WOM can be facilitated—made easier by certain techniques and tactics you employ—especially the one this entire book is about—which is our third Big Rule after:

1. **What's most important is not what people hear. It's what they <u>repeat</u>, after they've heard you.**

2. **Because you want to be transmitted via the new master medium—the <u>Word of Mouth Machines</u>.**

Now if those two are true, here's our next question. What type of message do they **want** to repeat?

BR 3:

What they want to repeat are <u>Micro-Scripts</u>

Remember *If the glove doesn't fit, you must acquit,* and *Nothing gets between me and my Calvins?* How many of you (us) have slyly winked when you said you were heading to Las Vegas and added, hey: *What happens in Vegas, stays in Vegas?*

Or for that matter, what did simple little words like the *Bridge to nowhere, He's a maverick* or *Toxic mortgages* mean to you before the fourth quarter of 2008? What did they mean to millions of people around the world just a few months later, including you and me?

These are **Micro-Scripts.** They are any set of words from one word to a sentence or two—no more than can fit on one Blackberry screen or the back of a T-shirt—that uses metaphors, descriptive imagery or just rhythmic words to verbalize an idea in a way that people like to say and to <u>repeat</u> to others. It's just enough information, just provocative enough to permit a person to act.

When people hear an idea or an instruction expressed in a Micro-Script, they're much more likely to pass it along in conversations, emails, blogs, press articles, text messages, even bumper stickers—any person-to-person communication that comes and goes quickly.

The Four Big Rules

You're going to see that Micro-Scripts are like magic words, used by master communicators in any field—politics, marketing, sales, academics, anything.

The reason is simple: they're messages verbalized in a way that's optimized for our heuristic brains. They work fast, let us absorb fast, decide fast, act fast—the way we like it. From now on, you'll need to understand their simple principles if you want your messages to break through. The truth is, they've been the secret of the really great communicators since time immemorial.

**Q: But isn't a Micro-Script just a
catch phrase or a sound bite?**

A: Sure—but it's much, much more—a
very special kind of sound bite.

It's a story bite.

It nearly always tells a whole story, provides a story piece or triggers one already running in the brain. It's used to inform, impress or influence—so it must contain just enough information to persuade another person to change a mind, or have permission to act. It is a bite that's designed to be repeated because people like to say it—and because it makes an impression on others when they do.

For example:

He's a flip-flopper! It's made from sugar to taste like sugar. Friends don't let friends drive drunk. It's finger-lickin' good. A diamond is forever.

If a sound bite, a tagline, even a descriptive name can do all the above, and if people are using it to tell others about you, then it meets the definition of a Micro-Script. Indeed, when a tagline is written like a Micro-Script, it's a much more effective tagline!

The key for any communicator is that once you have your big idea, learn to express it in Micro-Script.

The Gasoline for the Word of Mouth Machine

Micro-Scripts are also the best drivers of anything Word of Mouth or viral, which means they're the premium fuel for marketing in the new digital age.

Ironically, it's been the political campaigns (not the advertising industry that invented them) that have done some of the most impressive things to leverage the power of Micro-Scripts in recent years. After all, political campaigns are in constant clock-ticking, crisis-marketing mode by nature. As my friend Mark Walsh says: elections are a "one day sale for 100% market share." The Republicans figured it out with Ronald Reagan in the 80s (*Are you better off than you were four years ago?* and *There you go again!*) They were a decisive factor in five out of the seven presidential races that the GOP captured through 2004. The Democrats are just now catching up (*Yes we can!* and *McCain and Bush are McSame*).

But the smartest marketing communicators and brand people are finally re-figuring this out. And this book is here to show you that we can make Micro-Scripts for ourselves and our products and businesses, just as easily as they can.

So if 1) is "what's important is what people want to repeat," and 2) is "they'll do it on the Word of Mouth machines" and 3) "what they want to repeat are Micro-Scripts—" our last question is: what should be the *subject* of your Micro-Scripts? What should a Micro-Script be about?

That's our fourth Big Rule...

BR 4:
Build Them on Dominant Selling Ideas

The **Dominant Selling Idea** (DSI) is the ultimate value you're offering—the central proposition underlying any successful Micro-Script. The idea of a difference you're trying to communicate. Like speed, sexiness, strength or beauty—or a singular point of view. Since it's the Micro-Script foundation, it's always the first piece that needs to be in place before making our own Micro-Scripts—and it's going to be the first subject when we begin our deep dive in Part II of the book.

A Dominant Selling Idea is the <u>one</u> most unique, important and own-able advantage that you can claim that others don't—your single, best, differentiating attribute. In marketing textbook terms, it is brand positioning brought to its sharpest, most specific edge. *Safest car. The dentists' #1 toothpaste. The working man's favorite beer. The fastest headache pill. The longest-range jumbo jet.*

Only a few years ago it was considered a marketing ideal, the exclusive property of the great big consumer brands and a few smart practitioners on Madison Avenue (the former capital of advertising). Today it is every company's basic requirement in a tough environment—your strategic and tactical lifeline.

When we introduced the term Dominant Selling Idea a few years ago in *Why Johnny Can't Brand: Rediscovering the Lost Art of the Big Idea,* we thought the DSI was such an improved destination for most companies that if they got there, all the rest of branding and marketing could fall into place. It was the end chapter in the process.

Not any more. The hyper-connected, digital age showed us there's another crucial piece that's vital for communicators: the verbal expression that carries your Idea from one mind to the next.

That vessel is your Micro-Script—for the simplest of reasons:

People don't speak in strategy or concept, they speak in Micro-Script. They absorb in Micro-Script. If you want to put across your strategy then 1) sharpen it down to a Dominant Selling Idea and 2) verbalize that DSI in a Micro-Script.

One more time…

Rules of thumb tell our brains how to get to the heart of the matter fast, and automatically take the best action. They tell us to choose one Dominant Selling Idea and verbalize it in Micro-Scripts.

The **Dominant Selling Idea** is a central idea we want to communicate, a value that makes the difference. A superlative like the safest, fastest, easiest, strongest, or a simple point of view like "Guns aren't intrinsically bad."

A **Micro-Script** is the *verbal expression* of that core idea—in the concise, vivid, everyday words that human brains like; easy to remember and repeat.

When you take "Guns aren't intrinsically bad" and express it in Micro-Script, it comes out:

Guns don't kill people, people do.

One of the all-time greats.

Any important idea or directive—including a rule of thumb itself—can be made more powerful and memorable when verbalized as a Micro-Script.

What Micro-Scripts Say About Building Brands

Building Brands with Fewer, Simpler Elements—*from the Ground Up*—From Now On

In fat times, marketing people love devising big strategic solutions from "50,000 feet" that work on an intellectual scale. But in these times when ROI is "in" and budget wasting is "out," marketing people have to start thinking small—that is, from the ground up—a little more like salespeople. It's where the buying rubber meets the road in real life—the person-to-person, eye-level transaction place, whether it's seller-to-buyer, customer-to-call center, or person-to-package in the quiet and safety of the grocery aisle.

As ground-level persuasion creates sales, the notion of a "brand" will percolate upward more reliably than 50,000-foot strategies will trickle downward to create sales. The only way to get penetration in the hyper-conversation, is to start micro in order to get macro—to give every brain the working tools it loves to broadcast with.

We'll see later on that simple and "micro" will influence our whole approach to branding. The all-important "elevator pitch," for example, will be simplified, re-defined and re-vitalized as the *Micro-Pitch*.

All heuristics tell us this: at times of great uncertainty and complexity, think simple. Start small. In the new world, only if the brand works one-to-one, will it work one to a billion.

Hello, It's Your Mother

In the end, we're directed to the mother of today's commandments, not a rule as much as a guiding light if you're ever stuck in the process. An implicit philosophy. If the Micro-Script Rules reveal anything, it's that the more complex communication seems to be getting—the simpler and more unified it is actually becoming, as long as you keep in mind it's all just part of the ancient master medium. So if you ever veer off the path, just remember:

If you want to communicate in any medium, make it work first at the Word of Mouth level—ideally with Micro-Scripts—and you'll make it work on every level.

That is—

Make it work at Word of Mouth and you make it work.

Folks—if you stopped reading now and only remembered one thing, this is probably the thing. It might as well be the universal theory.

And we mean communications on any level, from building a global brand to a chat between two moms in the supermarket. If you can get it right at the level of a Word of Mouth exchange, you'll get it right.

Think about that for a second if you're sitting in a boardroom at a big corporation trying to strengthen your brand. Set your mind and your sights on making your messages work "over the backyard fence." In an elevator pitch that's *only one floor* long. It's the ultimate in high-yield marketing concepts. Your message must pass the Word of Mouth test or it's just not simple enough.

And to accomplish this? Start with the Four Big Rules.

Are You Ready?

"In ancient times when Cicero spoke, the people said 'how well he spoke.' But when Demosthenes spoke, they said, 'let us march.'" If that quote gets your heart beating a little faster, I know you're ready to heed the call.

Maybe the greatest wartime marketer of all, Winston Churchill, said this about challenging times:

If you're going through hell, keep going.

For all you wartime marketers reading this, that's what we're about to do.

Before we build our Micro-Script house, let's pour the foundation.

Remember The Four Biggest Rules are

1. <u>It's What They Repeat</u>—It's not important what they hear, it's what they want to *repeat* after they hear you.

2. <u>One Master Medium</u>—Remember now: *Every Screen's Just a Word of Mouth Machine.*

3. <u>Micro-Scripts</u>—What they *want* to repeat are *Micro-Scripts.*

4. <u>Dominant Selling Idea</u>—Micro-Scripts must be built on *DSIs.*

And the Mother Commandment is:

If You Make it Work at Word of Mouth Level, You'll Make it Work—Everywhere.

CHAPTER 2

Micro-Scripts

Say the Magic Words

...Nothing comes between me and my Calvins.
...What would Jesus do?
...No child left behind.
...Enterprise picks you up!
...Republicans are the party of "no."
...Think globally, act locally.
...Location, location, location.

Micro-Scripts are very short sets of magic words. Those "five or six words that can beat 5,000" we spoke of earlier. They are the key words we remember in order to repeat Dominant Selling Ideas, or any ideas, to ourselves and to others. Since the beginning of language, they are the ultimate vehicles for bringing DSIs to life and spreading them around. This makes them the active ingredient in "P2P" (Person-to-Person or Peer-to-Peer), that is, Word of Mouth and Viral Communication. It also makes them a catalyst for successful branding, marketing and selling communication in today's digital world and beyond. Micro-Scripts are words that actually change minds and persuade the undecided. To this day, visual as we think we are, words are still powerful enough to create hit movies, win elections, start wars or sell massive amounts of product. They put people into motion, not just into merriment. They are the best vehicle no matter what media you choose—including future channels we haven't even thought of. That's all they are.

So what are Micro-Scripts exactly so you can capture your own magic words?

Micro-Scripts Revealed
Let's Define Micro-Script

Here's the official definition:

A Micro-Script is a verbal "instant message" that people like to <u>repeat,</u> generally word-for-word, to inform, impress or persuade others. It lets the receiver make a snap judgment or take action on the least amount of information. It usually contains metaphors, vivid imagery or rhythmic sounds to form a complete idea in the mind. It's how to verbalize in the way that's optimized for the heuristic brain.

- It must be written in the simple way people speak— quick, compact and easy, short as a word or phrase.
- It must support your DSI if it's to be a marketing Micro-Script.
- It's a story bite because it either <u>tells a story</u> or provides a <u>story piece</u> or <u>triggers one</u> already running in the brain. We're wired to love and remember stories.

Again—the DNA in Micro-Scripts is pretty obvious. It conforms to our heuristic wiring. A Micro-Script is built the way it is to give the heuristic brain what it wants when it comes to hearing, absorbing, storing, retrieving and passing information along. And we ALWAYS want to give the brain what it wants.

Micro-Script Q&A:

Q: How is a Micro-Script Different than a Tagline or a Slogan?

A tagline—an anchoring slogan for an entity—can certainly be a Micro-Script if people also like to say it and repeat it to others. For example: People like and repeat the tagline for Las Vegas which supports the idea, "The adult playground designed to let you experience your fantasies without getting caught like you would at home in Cleveland." Instead, they tell you with a grin: *What happens in Vegas stays in Vegas.* They saw it on the TV commercial and they liked saying it to their friends. That's because the tagline is written in Micro-Script language that worked. *In general, any tagline that's written like a Micro-Script is a much more effective tagline.* In fact: Micro-Scripted taglines work like one-line elevator pitches, as we'll see later on. Nothing could be more valuable in today's hyperconnected world.

Q: How is a Micro-Script different than a Sound Bite?

A typical sound bite can be random, passive, picked up by the media for entertainment, shock, human interest. It may be empty of social or commercial importance. Doesn't matter.

But in a Micro-Script, the message is the whole point because it either tells a complete story, a piece of a story or it triggers one that's already teed up in the brain. It's purposely crafted as a persuasion and penetration tool, not just to be noticed, but to put others in motion, physically or mentally. Its specific, concentrated form is meant for easy broadcast by social media as well as paid media. But mostly human to human—that is, via the universal Word of Mouth Machines (all hand-held electronic devices) broadcasting from a palm near you. *No child left behind,* and *Bounty, the quicker picker upper* are not an accident. They are master-crafted. Designed to transmit. *Sarah Palin thought Africa was a country.* The entire electorate heard that in about 24 hours after it was first broadcast because it was a perfect Micro-Script.

Q: Aren't you talking about evil propaganda—using language to manipulate?

No, this isn't about value judgments. It's about the most effective human communication. The principles can be used for good or ill, so any communicator today must be certain to understand them. Today's digital Word of Mouth planet makes it more imperative than ever. If the opposition uses these weapons against you, you must arm yourself in kind— and use them for truth, justice and the righteous cause. Ask Abraham Lincoln, John F. Kennedy or Winston Churchill if you doubt this.

One Quick Thing About Metaphors...

...because they're so important to Micro-Scripts and story-telling in general.

A metaphor is simply describing one thing by likening it to another. Anything to anything, tangible or ethereal: *Love is blind. That dude's a rock. All the world's a stage.*

Basic as it is, it is our most powerful thought and language tool. And it's the core of what we'll call "Micro-Script language," i.e., rich with metaphor, vivid images, rhythmic patterns, descriptive and specific—the enemy of vague, generic and dull.

Linguists and psychologists have long known that metaphors are the way humans think, persuade, remember and organize thoughts. They are the building blocks of stories. *And stories are the secret to all great and lasting human communications*—sales, marketing, political, theatrical—everything. We're simply wired to absorb their sequence, rhythm and balance.

Metaphors cause the right brain to form hypnotic visualizations that go way beyond the metaphor itself, stimulating whole sets of personal associations, causing our story-loving brains to fill in the imaginary blanks. It's not uncommon to utter a metaphor to someone, and have it spontaneously trigger a whole monologue. Walk up to a group of women at a singles bar and ask any one to respond to these three words: "Men are wolves."

You don't have to be an English major to use metaphors. We all use them effortlessly in every conversation every day for instant color, context and comparison. This is why they're at the core of so many effective Micro-Scripts.

The Dynamic Difference

Finally—this a fundamental advantage to Micro-Scripts in the digital era:

A Micro-Script is a dynamic asset that's perfectly designed to operate in all the new media channels where communications are made and modified as fast as thumbs can text them. As long as it supports the DSI heart, a set of Micro-Scripts can easily evolve and have more iterations: *Airborne was invented by a second grade teacher to prevent colds. Airborne is used by flight attendants to keep from getting colds.* If it works, it proliferates. If it doesn't its discarded. What's important is that it adjusts on the fly—as opposed to traditional static elements like names or taglines, nailed onto the side of the building, which can't always keep up with the real-time conversation that marketing, political and social communication is becoming.

The traditional core elements like names and taglines are still crucial. Without solid anchors, there can be no brands. But winning is increasingly about adaptability and rapid response in today's dynamic marketing environment. Micro-Scripts are made to start fast and stay nimble.

CHAPTER 3

Real Micro-Scripts on Parade
A Brief Public History

Up next are some really famous Micro-Scripts in action to illustrate how it is possible to tell whole stories this way—sometimes in literally a word or two—and how powerful these little words can become. Just as important, we'll see that Micro-Scripts don't have to be famous or viral or cause a revolution to change your business or your life. Even the biggest and most famous has to work locally, first, to work at all. Their job is to impact the person next to you in that elevator, at the end of your text message, across from you at the boardroom table, in your sales presentation, or reading your website or your blog. Our job is to learn how to make Micro-Scripts that act *locally* so they can work globally.

Please heed this author's warning: There are no value judgments or political points intended by the following examples. They're here because they worked. Yes, Micro-Scripts can be used as propaganda and trickery in unscrupulous hands.

One of the most chilling, fear-inducing Micro-Scripts ever is the one that's been used by al-Qaida to sum up the new political and military equation in a terrorist world:

We love death more than you love life.

Nobody supports the terror criminals. But this incredible script has instilled fear around the world and tells a whole brutal story in eight words. It's a very effective Micro-Script—all the more reason that it's incumbent on ethical communicators to become experts at utilizing Micro-Script power to counter evil forces and advance the common good.

So let's get started with a visit to the Micro-Script Hall of Fame. Here you'll find diminutive collections of words that have had towering impact on civilizations and commercial fortunes. As I've said earlier—there's a ton to be learned from some of the recent ones created by political leaders, presidential candidates and sensational trial attorneys. Because with all that's involved today, the people who run campaigns or go for a big verdict are either great marketers, or dead in a very finite timeframe. You generally have six to eighteen months to make it work. You're in sales and marketing in a deep sense, often selling the intangible because your candidate's differences may not be discernible, at first, to the naked eye.

Everything Was Great Until "He Furloughed the Murderer"

This first one is here because it almost single-handedly changed a presidential election and therefore, history. In 1988, Mike Dukakis had a big lead going into the summer against

George H. W. Bush, a bland candidate who seemed hopelessly cast as a perennial runner-up. Dukakis had a PoliSci professor's grasp of the issues. He had language like: "We need bilateral cooperation to circumvent NATO's unilateralist tendencies, while avoiding the obstructionist dilemma."

Bush had a guy named Lee Atwater. Atwater wanted his gentlemanly boss to unleash him to use the opposite kind of language—the simple but gripping kind that an average American would absorb, remember and actually be able to repeat to someone who asked, "Why in the world are you for that wimp Bush?"

As the campaign headed for the home stretch, Bush let Atwater loose.

Suddenly a TV ad appeared. The mug shot of a convict named Willie Horton who was paroled while Dukakis was in office. Willie Horton had walked out of state prison, gone straight to Florida, and murdered a child. The Micro-Script that went along with the ad was *Dukakis—he furloughed the murderer.*

If you were worried about violent crime in America as most people were at the time, if you were on the fence about whether Dukakis might be an out-to-lunch, uber-liberal ideologue who'd make cock-eyed lefty decisions in the White House as the Republicans claimed—it penetrated. And it was passed around like a ricocheting bullet.

I'm from Massachusetts too, and back then Dukakis was our governor. I can't remember a single word or phrase Dukakis said in that campaign. But more than twenty years later I remember people coming up to me and saying: *"You know, he furloughed that murderer, Willie Horton."*

For those who wanted an environmental issue, they ran the ad: "He says he's for a clean environment but '*He polluted the harbor.*'"

Now, all Bubba in Biloxi or Harry in Hartford had to remember if he wanted to defend his position or impress a neighbor was four words—with confidence:

He furloughed the murderer or *He polluted the harbor.* He's a liberal fool.

Dukakis lost. Bush won. To historians, those ads and Micro-Scripts were a turning point. Fair or not, they were magic words.

It Worked in Reverse the Next Time—But Still Worked

Micro-Scripts work just as well to sell you or un-sell the competition as negative ads like the Willie Horton attest. And once a good one's installed, it doesn't just go away. Before the next election, George Bush went around saying: "*Read my lips. No new taxes.*" It was an unforgettable line. He branded himself as the no-tax guy. People remembered it and said it and liked it a lot.

Then the economy made him raise taxes. People still remembered it and said it and liked it. But now Bush became a victim of his own Micro-Script. Now it meant he was wishy-washy and ineffective. That—plus James Carville's Micro-Script for Clinton that the press picked up and publicized—*It's the economy, stupid*—did Bush in.

Until There Was...The *Flip-flopper*

But the Democrats amazingly, still hadn't learned. So in 2000 Al Gore got tarred by the opposition with the mocking *He says he invented the Internet* and other classics. While Bush won with Micro-Scripts like *He's the compassionate conservative.* But the granddaddy was saved for John Kerry in 2004. Kerry and his brilliant consultants had him back talking like Dukakis used to; in eastern patrician, Ivy League words and syntax only a policy wonk could love. What average Joe or working single mom could forget a stirring phrase like: "A bold, progressive internationalism that stands in stark contrast to the too often belligerent and myopic unilateralism of the Bush administration."

You're right, all of them.

Then Kerry gave the Republican Micro-Script machine a gift-wrapped Christmas present. He said: *"I was for it before I was against it."* The Republicans thanked him for providing his own gem for them to use—then raised it to: *He's a flip-flopper.*

It was a mind changer, a momentum changer and a game changer. Kerry was professionally boxed and framed. The news media picked it up in minutes and it entered the language literally within hours—and by the way that was <u>before</u> texting and universal high-speed Internet. From Ketchikan to Kennebunkport, people who might never read the paper or be able to quote you a single policy fact, could tell you instantly in response to anything: "Well, I don't want a President who's a *flip-flopper.*"

"Flip-flopper" was actually fun to say. It had rhythm and alliteration. It was quick. It conjured up preconceived stories of phony, say-anything politicians, lack of principles, untrustworthiness—as weak and pathetic as a flopping fish in the bottom of your boat. A Hall of Fame Micro-Script.

That year, I actually got tickets to the Republican National Convention in New York City. Every time a speaker would get around to Kerry's record, the place would erupt spontaneously with "FLIP-FLOP-PER, FLIP-FLOP-PER!" and take a minute or two to quiet down. They'd wave little plastic beach flip-flops. The podium couldn't shut them off.

Kerry lost by a percentage point. Republican brilliance and Democratic utter ignorance of language and thought dynamics (metaphors and Micro-Scripts) made a critical difference. The Republicans had used magic words.

Finally, a liberal professor and linguist from U.C. Berkeley named George Lakoff had heard enough. He wrote a book in 2004 called *Don't Think of an Elephant!* to wake the Democrats up to the Republican monopoly on mesmerizing words and phrases that had been skewering them for decades. *Death tax* vs. Estate tax. *Tax relief* vs. Tax cuts. And *No child left behind.*

By 2008 Democrats were coming up with effective Micro-Scripts of their own. They laid out script after script in speeches and on their interactive website and stuck to the positive *(Yes We Can!)* and negative ones that worked—scripts like *Bush and McCain are McSame. John McCain is running for Bush's third term.* They discarded those that failed. They mined their own supporters and the media for inspired new Micro-Scripts as well. By keeping fast and fluid—responding quickly to counter very crafty attempts to light Micro-Script fires around Obama like *Do we really know who he is...* and *He's a socialist,* the Democrats refused to let themselves be caught, *flip-floppered* or *swift-boated.**

---

* In Chapter 9, I'll give some specifics on how to out-Micro-Script your rivals when you find yourself under attack.

There is no doubt that the Democrats had massive social and political unrest on their side, an unpopular war and an economic downturn. Micro-Scripting didn't do it alone, of course. But there is no doubt Micro-Scripts helped lift the most unlikely of candidates past Hillary Clinton first and a war hero next. If nothing else, this time they kept the Democrats from snatching defeat from a sure victory.

History Changers

When I visited Vietnam recently, I went to the war museums there. Exhibits are often illustrated with magazine and newspaper clippings of the time, so I was constantly reminded of the great refrain which turned out to be one of history's most tragically successful Micro-Scripts:

The Domino Theory

For those too young to recall, the domino theory was a Micro-Script that explained an entire foreign policy in two words. During the Cold War, it was the reigning metaphor used to justify military action, defense budgets and eventually an entire war in Southeast Asia costing millions of lives. It persuaded us that the communists were a giant conspiracy, so that once one nation fell, the nation next to it would fall and so on—just like falling dominos. All the way to Ohio.

Pretty much any American of grade school age could understand and repeat the words "domino theory." What a Micro-Script! Say-able, metaphorical, logical, memorable, with a clear point of view. When Washington decided to go to full scale war to stop the dominos in Vietnam, the nation was philosophically ready. The phrase was magic.

Except it wasn't true.

We realized later that the Vietnamese thought of themselves as a distinct nation, no more likely to be a communist "domino" than a French or American one. They'd been fighting off invaders for more than 3,000 years. The domino theory wasn't true in Europe either. In fact, the reverse Domino was true. As one country after another kicked out the communists in the 80s, they all went back to being their own independent national selves again. No nation ever wanted to be someone else's domino. But that amazing Micro-Script, running in our collective Cold War brains, gave us the logic and the permission to make one of the greatest foreign policy mistakes in history. The image was just too powerful to resist.

A Few Others—They All Work More or Less the Same Way

Guns don't kill people, people do. I've got to mention this one again because it's so powerful. It's been used for decades to instantly frame, inform, influence and rally Americans against gun control. It's not a tagline. It's on bumper stickers, used in conversations, speeches and arguments. Its simple logic is unassailable and it provides you with an entire argument in six words, whether you agree with it or not.

The *Bridge to nowhere.* I was at the site of the bridge to nowhere. It wasn't to nowhere—it was the bridge the government promised the people of Ketchikan Alaska if they put the new airport and industrial properties on an island off the coast—the only place the city had to expand. It's the fourth largest city in Alaska. They have hundreds of thousands of visitors a year. It would cost less than one modern Air Force bomber. It was the bridge to the airport. Then someone coined the Micro-Script. It became an instant sensation as far as the Florida Keys. An unforgettable metaphoric symbol of Washington waste, greed, stupidity and corruption. The bridge was as good as dead. Magic words did this.

And one of my personal favorites as a skydiver:

Why would anyone jump out of a perfectly good airplane?

I've had monks from Tibet tell me that. Dying patients whisper it to me as their last words with the most satisfied look on their face. It's a Micro-Script that's known and said the world round. The question on this one is, why? I think it just makes the person saying it feel sharper than the irresponsible few who would ever even consider skydiving. It's a completely nifty bit of wordsmanship that sums up an entire argument and presumably wins it on logic—an open-and-shut case—in ten tight little words. That's a conversational opportunity you want to seize when you get it. So people have fun saying it and being superior to you if you're a skydiver or anyone they think they're enlightening with this (smug) pearl of wisdom.

Now here's an entire 244-page bestselling book, reduced to seven words:

Eat food, not too much, mostly plants.

It's important to remember that a great Micro-Script doesn't *always* have to be built on an obvious central metaphor, nor does it have to be known to millions. It qualifies if it contains or triggers a whole idea, is compact, memorable and if people want to repeat it to their friends.

Any one of the thousands of people who've read Michael Pollan's wonderful book on food and nutrition called *In Defense of Food* will be able to repeat the seven-word mantra found in the first sentence of the first page: *Eat food, not too much. Mostly plants.* (Pollan actually apologized that he'd just given away the entire book in those first seven words and now needed to find a way to fill the other 200 pages!) I have told it to people a hundred times as I recommend the book. I use it to remind myself every day. Every facet, except the "Not too much" part.

And maybe you've heard or said...

Carnival—they're the FUN ships.

Size doesn't matter.

He's just not that into you.

The ultimate driving machine.

Just say no.

Crest is recommended by dentists.

It's good to the last drop.

She can see RUSSIA from her HOUSE!

Or this last one...

Later on in the book you're going to see that you can create Micro-Scripts for any important idea you have to communicate. Some people try to give me excuses. "Oh, my product or service is too complex," they say. My reply to that is, "Oh, really?"

Because I know a little story about a famous Talmudic scholar who was asked once if he could explain the Bible.

He replied: "Yes, and I can tell you in one sentence:

'Do unto others as you'd have others do to you.' All the rest is commentary."

To any Micro-Script naysayers or nervous Nellies out there who doubt that it can be done for their idea, I say that *if the whole Bible can be told in ten words,* or a Hemingway novel (see Chapter 6), well, there's a pretty good chance we should be able to communicate something like our product or service concept or corporate mission or positioning statement, don't you think? In fact, if we can't, that's a pretty good indication that something more fundamental is wrong with the idea itself. It needs more focus.

Where Your Micro-Scripts Will Play
Micro-Messaging Across The Board...

In sales presentations, advertising, mission statements, websites, blogs, PR—Micro-Scripts are the potent content we'll use wherever we want our ideas told or sold because they are perfectly packaged selling ideas, formatted the way our heuristic brains like it for instant filing and retrieval at high speed. They get us to market quickly and inexpensively, after we secure our

Dominant Selling Idea, that is. They are a universal, bottom line, communication language—fuel for the Word of Mouth Machine that will ultimately shape and define our brand.

Finding Your Own Micro-Scripts

First off, we'll look at commercial examples, a few more case histories to deepen our understanding of how these things are put together. Then in Part II, we'll cover the specific process of beginning to do it, now.

Remember These Micro-Script Rules

1. Always make it work the way the heuristic brain likes to work. *For key ideas, use Micro-Scripts and Micro-Script language.*

2. A Micro-Script is designed *to inform, impress or persuade others.*

3. Micro-Scripts contain *metaphors, vivid imagery or rhythmic sounds* to trigger a complete idea in the mind with the least number of words.

4. *A rule of thumb, a tagline, a Dominant Selling Idea or even a name can be expressed in Micro-Script language.* It's a Micro-Script if people like to repeat it. It makes any expression more powerful.

5. Always build your Micro-Script on a *Dominant Selling Idea*—if you want to sell a product or build a brand.

6. Micro-Scripts will play wherever ideas are told and sold.

CHAPTER 4

Micro-Scripts for You and Me

Just a few little words, the right words, can change your world, no matter how big and global or how small and local your world happens to be. It's what they meant by the classic Micro-Script—*there's nothing more powerful than an idea whose time has come.* Because the "idea could only come" via the spoken, and sometimes written, word. It still does. Video and imaging no doubt play a crucial role in conveying and augmenting ideas today. But Micro-Script rules of thumb are as true as ever including this one: *the idea that's say-able is always more playable.* The more concise you find you can make it, the stronger you'll know your idea is and vice versa. If you can't say it simply and cogently, it's not quite there yet. And that goes for branding and selling ideas no matter what.

The familiar examples we started with like *Bridge to nowhere* were done by political communicators who rank among today's most skilled at deploying Micro-Scripts. But their objectives match with ours: reach the widest target audience with the most penetrating message for the least money in the shortest time. Or else.

What we need to do today is rather obvious, isn't it? Get your hands on these little babies as quickly as possible and put them to work. Find some magic words so that everyone can sing your Dominant Selling Idea.

The Micro-Script as Mar/Com (Marketing Communications)

Remember—if somebody loves your product, they will love to tell others about it for all kinds of reasons. Furnish them with a nifty set of words and they'll love you even more and be happy to deploy them for their own conversational gain.

Look at how efficient a tool you're giving your customers who love your artificial sweetener and want to tell others about it:

It's made from sugar so it tastes like sugar...

Think about the immensity of the story contained in those eight words: it's safe and natural, not chemical, it has the least artificial taste, it has credible sugar qualities that make it better for cooking and recipes, I can feel good about it, not fearful or guilty, my family will appreciate me for it. I can remove sugar from my life without suffering, with less stigma. There are probably a billion personal stories that come into play with those eight little words. The metaphor is simply: *Splenda is sugar.*

Now, for Splenda this Micro-Script proved to be so powerful, they ended up using this exact version as their tagline.

But in saying it, people would develop their own Micro-Script variations—all on strategy, all okay. When I used to recommend Splenda in my no-carb, no-sugar halcyon days, I'd say: "It's made from sugar so…it has the most natural sugar taste"; and/or "it even looks like little sugar granules"; and/or "you can bake with it just like regular sugar and it doesn't clump up."

But Splenda was smart enough in the beginning to furnish me with the sweetest little phrase that played to me, persuaded me, and then was endlessly say-able by me to all my low-carb-I-hate-fake-sugar friends.

Splenda as we know rocketed to about a 50% share of the market within three years or so of being introduced. Never mind that their desperate competitors launched and won a lawsuit that claimed false advertising, since "made from sugar" turned out to be technically…a stretch. The scientist who accidently discovered Splenda was trying to invent a new insecticide, no kidding. But that wouldn't have been that good a Micro-Script to use.

Since there was some derivation of a sugar molecule in the original formula, voilà! They made the famous claim. The courts eventually forced them to modify the explicit "made from sugar" language.

But the Splenda Micro-Scripts had already done their magic. Now, on the side of the packet, Splenda winks and smartly says: *Just What's Good.*

That's purely an advertising tagline, not a Micro-Script— but we know what they mean. They're still right smack on the Dominant Selling Idea: *the most natural-tasting sweetener.* And it just keeps triggering the original Micro-Script in my head which is the gift that keeps on giving.

"They Call It a Journey"

I just heard this one and it's brilliant. Have you seen those diamond necklaces that are just one long, wavy line of six or seven stones that hang vertically from a simple chain—the diamonds get larger toward the bottom?

I see them everywhere. The young lady who cuts my hair had one. I said that's nice, I've seen those and she stopped, touched it and said dreamily: "My boyfriend bought it for me. *He said it's called it a 'Journey…'*"

A Journey, huh? I know her boyfriend Anthony who works construction didn't make that up.

He used this one word Micro-Script when he handed it to her—a romantic reference to the winding road of love. It made him sound eloquent and attuned to the stirrings of the feminine heart. The smart jewelers furnished it for him and he was more than happy to pass it on. It imbued the piece with a deeper, unforgettable meaning.

The journey took him straight to her heart.

"Pork is the Other White Meat"

What a great selling line. I know because the waiter used it on me the other night to close me on the pork cutlet special instead of the fish or chicken. I told him, I bet it's good but I'm trying to eat lean. And he said, "Yeah but it IS lean. Don't you know:

Pork is the other white meat.

It's leaner than you think. It's the bacon you gotta stay away from."

Of course I'd heard it before too, but his little reminder was the permission I needed at that moment to buy what I really wanted. It was good, too.

"Enterprise Picks You Up"

Again, it's a full-fledged Micro-Script if it's repeated by people—and that includes you, recommending it to all your friends when they need a rental car. If I ask nearly anyone whether they like Enterprise, they'll repeat: *"Well they do pick you up."*

That's not important at the airport, but it sure is when my car's in the shop and I need a rental for a couple of days.

You have to give the company credit for sticking with this Dominant Selling Idea turned into a simple Micro-Script, used when they pick up the phone, in their advertising copy, and on their website for so long. They say it and we say it. It's all the information you need to understand exactly what differentiates them when you're in the market.

By the way—on the strength of this DSI-based Micro-Script and the non-airport distribution strategy that went with it—Enterprise's revenues got to the point where they actually exceeded Hertz.

But They Don't Have to be Famous!

You don't have to be a famous company or have a giant ad budget like Enterprise. Remember—a great Micro-Script works on one person at a time as well as it works on a million. If you've got a product that people want, it'll get you famous faster. So *Think locally to act globally.*

Here are some real-life examples:

An ATM in Every Home

There was no greater Micro-Script lesson for me personally than this one. I was lucky enough to help start a company that built a real product and prospered during the dot.com bubble. (Of course, we didn't call them Micro-Scripts then.)

We were building the first easy-to-use software for banking at home on your PC. All our competitors—Quicken, Microsoft Money and at the time VISA—were *saying* their products were easy. But to most people who don't even balance their checkbooks in real life, they were complex, hard to learn and intimidating. In fact, bought with all the right intentions, half of these products never made it out of the shrink wrap. Not a recipe for mass uptake. The banks wanted easy.

Ours WAS easy. But we found out quickly that big banks weren't excited about doing business with or even listening to five-person companies like ours.

Until we found a metaphor and turned it into a couple of Micro-Scripts that were simply...irresistible. Not only to buyers but to the trade press, which helped a lot.

We said: "Our software is called Home ATM. It looks just like your bank's branded ATM on their home computer. In fact it's so simple: if you know how to use an ATM, you know how to do home banking. It doesn't even need a manual!"

– *It's called Home ATM.*

– *It's like having your bank's ATM in every home.*

– If you can use an ATM, you already know how to use it.

– It's so simple, it doesn't even have a manual!

Four Micro-Scripts (including the name) that changed the lives of everyone in that company, because from then on we were never turned down for a meeting. Buyers got it, they remembered it, they were intrigued by it, and they wanted to see it. They told others about it in conferences. Because they could talk about it: *"Have you seen that product that works like an ATM?"*

In three years, we had more than 150 employees and sold the brand to a New York Stock Exchange company.

And it Worked Across the Business

The Micro-Script worked for us on the outbound sales calls, in our advertising, on our website and in the press. It would have worked in a text message just as well.

Micro-Pitch vs. Elevator Pitch

In fact, string a series of scripts together the way we did and you'll get something much more succinct, more cogent and tight than the average "elevator pitch." We had ourselves a **Micro-Pitch**, made by linking together our powerful, easy to remember and persuasive scripts. Anybody in the company could remember it and say it. It was the story pieces, assembled into the story.

This notion of the Micro-Pitch is such a powerful and effective one, it gets its own treatment in our How-To Part II later in the book.

McMenamy's Fish Market

Unbelievable. I just Googled McMenamy's Seafood as I was writing this and there it is still! With its motto. But McMenamy's is way bigger now than when I was a kid. All fish markets have the word "fresh" on their signs. All of them, always. So the word has become invisible for most fish markets. But McMenamy's was famous far and wide (in the Boston area) for a unique slogan—a Micro-Script indeed because anyone who'd ever been there, never failed to remind you of it with a grin.

I'm copying this off the Internet now, but I heard it first from my friend John Powers before personal computers were invented…

> *At McMenamy's…The fish you buy today,*
> *swam last night in Buzzard's Bay!*

Even today, if someone asked me to mention the name of a fish market or a seafood place, one always comes to mind first. McMenamy's keeps reminding me they have the freshest fish and they don't even say the word "fresh"! They do it with a story bite—eleven words with specific, colorful imagery, a little attitude and a little rhythm that people like to say. And that sets them apart.

Micro-Scripts for Sales

> *Paint a picture, then put your prospect inside it.*
> —Famous sales advice told in a Micro-Script, *Anon.*

All-star sales communicators tell stories. And the key selling points in their stories are packaged for easy takeaway in Micro-Scripts. Some do it naturally because they have a gift. But most aren't natural wordsmiths. They listen to the Micro-Scripts of other superstars, or the vivid phrases of their customers, and use those. The buyer doesn't care where it comes from.

Here's what recently happened to me.

I'd been talking for two years about buying a convertible. I like Volvos as perhaps you can already tell from all my references to the DSI "Safe Car." I was at the dealer's one day, waiting for a repair on my Volvo wagon when there it was... the new C70 *hardtop* convertible! It was gorgeous. The hardtop solved the little convertible objections I had, like bad visibility when the top's down, and not wanting to drive a rag-top around all winter. I wanted a year-round car.

So I asked the salesman to show me how the top went up and down. It was nifty—but then pop—my caution flags went up. It seemed like it had a million little moving parts! Springs and levers and bearings and hatches that had to open and close. As a pilot and a skydiver, it's kinda drilled into me to beware of moving parts because every one is an opportunity to malfunction. Less is definitely more when it comes to moving parts. So I said to this salesman: "Looks like a lotta things that can break." And he said, "Hey, toys always cost more..."

Pffffhhhhttt (air going out of a balloon): Buying impulse dead. Just like that.

But I always had my eye on that car. I kinda hoped someone would change my mind. And then a year later, at another dealership, I met Sam. And here's what Sam said when I said, "Looks like a lotta moving parts, huh?"

He said, "Yes, you'd think so but *actually* the technology hasn't changed:

It's the same mechanics as a rag-top with *three hard pieces* (Micro-Script #1)

I said rea-l-l-l-l-y? And then he said: "Volvo really tested this…

They cycled it <u>over a million times</u>. (Micro-Script #2)

If you cycled it twice a day, it'd take *you <u>a thousand years</u>!* (Micro-Script #3)

No kiddin'.

Those simple scripts—put together in a quick Micro-Pitch—were as lovely to me as that car. I went home and *happily repeated* them to my neighbor. I mentioned them to my brother. They cycled in my brain over a million times. I was sold. And I would have bought it too, if only I hadn't mentioned it to my wife.

The interesting thing is that Sam didn't make them up. He picked them up from another seller. Any salesperson could've used those Micro-Scripts as convincingly as Sam and sold me that car. Those things are portable and scalable!

If I was the sales manager with fifty salespeople, I'd give those Micro-Scripts to all fifty and watch them make more sales.

Then again if I had fifty people with Blackberries and a couple of Micro-Scripts like that…it works the same way.

Here's the best Micro-Script about good salesmanship I ever heard. The top insurance salesperson for New York Life told me this:

If all it takes to make the sale is say 'Boo,' don't say 'Boo Boo.'

He said it, I laughed and never forgot it. Shut up when the buyer says yes. Novices keep talking anyway and un-sell the sale. I've told it to everyone I've ever presented with, as much so they'll remind me when I go on too long. When I hear my colleague start "coughing" (bu-hoo, boob-hoo) and kicking me under the table, I know I'm doing Boo Boo. It's a rule of thumb, packed in a fun little Micro-Script.

No One Gets More Immediate Micro-Script Mojo Than Salespeople!

People who do live selling get a remarkable advantage that marketers and copywriters don't. They're in a dynamic Micro-Script laboratory on every sales call. They not only get to match their scripts to different individuals based on the buyer's personality, interests, wants and needs—they get to test-market and refine new ones on the fly—using what works and discarding what doesn't. They can pick up an arsenal of super persuasion from other great salespeople and develop their own. They'll use Micro-Scripts for answering objections, presenting, closing, anything. Because they work.

This is anything but rote, machine-like or manipulative behavior. It's a tool kit of the trade. And great language, great logic and great stories and anecdotes are tools of the sales professional. If anything, they free you up to be more creative, not less.

Micro-Scripts help salespeople persuade customers and help you persuade salespeople how to be better salespeople.

Perhaps the most famous and successful sales training program in American history is the Dale Carnegie course. Every beginning student was given this single magic Micro-Scripted approach, proven over decades, to persuade reluctant, busy, uninterested prospects to do the impossible: give you a minute's attention to hear your pitch. It was a script that a rational person couldn't say no to. Instead, they pretty much had to respond, "What is it?"

If there was a way to (get a specific value, minus risk)—
you'd want to know about it, wouldn't you?

If there was a way to lower your monthly costs by 40% without
buying any new equipment, you'd want to know about it wouldn't you?

It was just that simple. It was a scripted gift that you knew would instantly turn you into a salesperson who actually had a chance. You used it happily the first time you could. I know master salespeople who've used nothing more than variations on that approach for their entire careers.

Dr. Donald Moine and Dr. Kenneth Lloyd, both Ph.Ds in psychology, wrote a book a few years back called *Unlimited Selling Power* in which they explained the natural, hypnotic, metaphor-laced speech patterns that superstar salespeople use to sell five times, ten times, a hundred times more than everybody else. But most importantly for all the rest of us with unremarkable talent and charisma, he went on to show how copying and scripting the superstars' hypnotic speech could boost any average salesperson's effectiveness in almost any situation, immediately.

Don Moine was often contracted by sales companies to build what he called "Mastermind Script Books" that could be duplicated and distributed to the sales force.

How they were compiled was actually quite simple. Moine would get permission to interview the very top sellers at length, follow them on sales calls, and tape-record their exact words and phrasing.

The book would be tabbed and organized with everything from answers to the most common objections to features, benefits and closes.

For each big objection, there might be fifteen different ways to answer.

Here's a classic:

Pretend you're working for a company making outbound calls. I'll give you two seconds. How do you answer the ultimate, flat objection:

I'm not interested!

If you stammer or protest, the phone is on its way to hang up in second three.

Or you could borrow a script:

> **There is no reason on earth** why you should be
> interested in our product until I can show you how
> it can help you make money, increase productivity

and solve some of your problems. CAN I SHOW YOU HOW WE CAN ACCOMPLISH THAT?

Or the next one in the script book:

I'm not interested!

Well sir, seventy business executives have bought this product over the last two weeks and they **all** began by saying they were not interested. They only bought because they found it could save them money and cut down on their headaches. Would you like to learn what they learned?[6]

Kind of beautiful isn't it. Now you almost can't wait for some shmoe to say: *"I'm not interested,"* can you?

The point here is that if you give any person a well-scripted phrase to say and they think saying it will make them be smarter, more effective or more successful in whatever they're trying to pass along, they'll say it.

A good objection-answering script would only be shared or go "viral" within the boundaries of your sales force. But hand out DSI Micro-Scripts like the Volvo convertible or the ones for Home ATM, and it'll go to the buyer, then to decision influencers, then to friends, or bosses or champions in an organization in a positive progression.

Incidentally, Don Moine and Ken Lloyd became friends of mine. I hadn't seen Don in years, until I saw him quoted in, are you ready...*The Tipping Point* by Malcolm Gladwell!

I'm not paranoid but...doesn't it seem like Malcolm is following me around?

PR Communications
It's more important than ever to use Micro-Scripts in PR. For *all* the same reasons.

Remember

1. *The idea that's say-able is always more play-able...*
    You don't need to be rich or famous. Anyone
    with an idea and a person to tell it to can create
    a Micro-Script.

2. No place is it more important than *sales* and PR
    to provide and practice Micro-Scripts.

Part II

Create, Capture, Convert

Introduction to Part II

We've got to quickly take care of first things first before we dive into the actual mechanics of making Micro-Scripts. That means I'm going to summarize our previous 263-page book on the Dominant Selling Idea—*Why Johnny Can't Brand: Rediscovering the Lost Art of the Big Idea,* in the next chapter for you. To create great Micro-Scripts, we've got to be dead certain of our DSI, our central, differentiating idea—the one we're going to turn into Micro-Scripts.

If you're already expert in the Dominant Selling Idea and don't need any refresher, go ahead and skip the next chapter.

Otherwise, I want to ask you this:

How Many Hearts Do You Have?

Not a trick question. Conventional wisdom says that we have *one.*

How many hearts can your brand or your idea or your message have if you want it to break through in this world? The answer is *One.*

Finding and nurturing this heart is the one and only heart of the matter. In branding, marketing and sales it's called your **Dominant Selling Idea**—*your DSI*. In challenging economies and the burgeoning digital world, the mere existence of this heart decides whether your brand's a killer whale or a jellyfish in the food chain. Whether you're communicating en masse or face to face, the most successful brands and effective presentations have a DSI beating at the center.

So you must immediately make an assessment: do you have a strong, obvious DSI, an anemic one, or none at all and need to get one fast?

Let's find out.

CHAPTER 5

Setting Your Foundation

Dominant Selling Idea 101: One Heart, One Soul

Great value propositions have one thing in common: **One Thing.** A single, big promise that is the big takeaway—what sets you apart from all others. Not two, not five features jammed into a paragraph. <u>One</u> attribute, one advantage that's most important to the target that you do best. *Safest* tire. *Fastest* human. *The only* shoes that breathe. That kind of thing.

The One Item of Carry-On Rule

Why is having one idea so important and not a long list of features and benefits the customer can choose from? It's because of a DSI heuristic we call the *One Item of Carry-on Rule*—the rule that says that in a world where we're bombarded by a trillion messages a day, people tend to remember one key thing about you if you're lucky enough for them to remember anything at all.

When you dump a pile of information on anyone, they'll simply pick out the one idea that's most important to them for whatever reason, and put it up in the overhead bin. All the rest gets left at the curb. That's because we instantly, instinctively surmise what we think is the heart of the matter and choose to retain it. There's simply too much other information to file for us not to prioritize in this way. Once upon a time, it was a matter of survival.

So it stands to reason as communicators, we'd want our customers to carry on the single most unique, important and own-able idea we can find—the one big thing that differentiates us from all the others.

A Dominant Selling Idea is simply this "one big thing" value proposition where the key advantage is literally the difference that makes you buy *this one* vs. that one. The tipping point that drives the sale. It tells the world, you're the *only*, the *most*, the *best*, or the *number one* choice in their price range.

For those of you familiar with the marketing term "positioning," the Dominant Selling Idea is your positioning, brought to its sharpest, most defined point.

Everyone Goes for the Top Draft Choice

This idea of "one-ness" is really important for another reason. Because if you think about it, we never set out to purchase the second-, third- or fourth-best solution to any problem. At the moment of purchase truth, we make a decision for only one product: the winner in our mind's eye—the best in the most important metric in that category that we can afford at that moment. It can be any **one** of a hundred attributes: the fastest, the healthiest, the most durable, the most reliable, the most attractive, the most sexy, the safest, the most prestigious, the largest, the strongest, the lightest, the best priced, the cheapest priced, most energy efficient, the most authentic, the softest or the hardest. So in a world with endless choices and hyper-communication, with millions of features adding up to a barrage of sameness—our first order of business as communicators is to find the one unique, important and own-able "best" that sets us apart. It's what puts buyers in action, to reach out for one item on the shelf, pick up the phone or get out of the chair.

That will be your Dominant Selling Idea.

You Can Have All the Great Supporting Attributes You Want

I'm not saying that you won't have a number of other excellent, attractive features and benefits that support the sale. All good products do. But the objective is to be an obvious standout in one attribute of highest importance to your audience. That's your calling card that gets inserted with a tab sticking up in the file cabinet of the brain. Being thought of as "best" at something important to the customer is the *only* position worth having. If you're not now the best in your category or specialty—you'll need to define a new specialty to claim #1 in. Don't worry—it's done every day in branding and we'll show you how.

Seeing the DSIs All Around Us

They're everywhere. You know them. And the more you look, the more a great number of brand communications will be conspicuous by their DSI absence. In the days when TV and radio were king, advertisers were brilliant at culling out and expressing the Dominant Selling Idea, many of which have lasted for generations. We all know these classics. The DSI is underlined:

> M&Ms...The little chocolate pellets, that come with a shiny shell in pretty colors so <u>the chocolate doesn't rub off and make a mess</u>...

> Wheaties... cereal so nutritious, it <u>makes you a winning athlete</u>...

> Hall's Throat Lozenges...the one's with unique, <u>nose clearing menthol fumes</u>...

> Timex Watches—the <u>most durable watches</u>...

Whoooops—quick time out—

We need to interject something right here because it illustrates a fundamental point so well...

Wasn't your mind interrupting and tugging at you just now when you read the DSIs for those great brands? After M&Ms, wasn't your mind saying, "No, idiot, it *Melts in your mouth not in your hand*." Didn't it shout, "*Wheaties: Breakfast of Champions*." And come onnnnn, everyone knows that *"Timex takes a lickin' and keeps on tickin'!"* Because that's the way your mind remembers them and likes saying them.

My friends, what your brain wanted to sing like a song were the great Micro-Scripts that were created to express those Dominant Selling Ideas, written by craftsmen more than sixty years ago. They wrote Micro-Scripts like *Breakfast of Champions* to install their ultimate value propositions—their DSIs—in our brains. And it worked so well we couldn't uninstall them now, even if we tried. The DSI for Allstate Insurance might've been a bland superlative like "the insurance company you trust most to protect you." But the *Micro-Script* for that DSI was *You're in good hands with Allstate.* And yes, in these particular cases, the Micro-Scripts were so powerful and effective, they were summoned to work as the brand taglines, too. As we've said, there's no reason a Micro-Script can't be deployed as a tagline if it expresses a complete idea, memorably spoken.

Don't forget that a Dominant Selling Idea is the objective advantage itself. The Micro-Script is its verbal *expression*—done in the vivid, descriptive way that makes it easy to remember and repeat to others.

Okay, back to DSI basic training.

The Smartest Marketers are Doing it Still

Many criticize the modern purveyors of substance-less marketing communication—but there are still superstars who emerge with excellent, clear DSIs and have the meteoric market share to show for it.

Here are some current DSI-based brands you've probably noticed:

Splenda—the <u>non-artificial low-calorie sweetener</u>

Geox Shoes—The first shoes that have <u>ventilation in the soles</u>.

Kashi Products—The <u>unique whole grain blend</u> in every product.

Geico—the car insurance that's <u>15% cheaper</u>.

Flowers.com—the flowers that come <u>directly from the field</u> so they're fresher.

These DSIs above are gift-wrapped and handed to you on a silver platter, not only because they're simple but because they are relentlessly consistent. Their beauty is undeniably functional. For the most part, we can't even say their names without simultaneously thinking of the selling idea attached—and vice versa. We call that the gift that keeps on giving.

It is of no small consequence that these brand marketers—smart enough to choose and stick to a DSI for their products in the first place, also furnished their loyal users with succinct, Micro-Scripted language to make their DSIs memorable and repeatable:

> Splenda—*made from sugar so it tastes like sugar* (rhythmic metaphor)
>
> Geox—*the shoes that breathe* (a powerful visual metaphor)
>
> Kashi—*7 whole grains on a mission* (specific, human-quest metaphor)
>
> Geico—*15 minutes saves you 15%* (specific, rhythmic, time-is-money metaphor)

There's an amazing amount of selling information contained in every one.

Now of course, you can do this, too. Here are a few other DSIs I spotted just by driving down Route 1:

The *fastest outboard engine*, the *real New York-style bagel place* (in Bangor, Maine), the *unbreakable line of laptops*, the *highest mileage hybrid*, the *online dating website for lawyers*, the *only organic local farmer's market*, and the *Shoreline's shoulder surgery specialty group*.

I hope you're seeing that it's not brain surgery. It's brain *singularity*.

You Can Spot DSIs in Names

If you have a simple and clear Dominant Selling Idea, it can appear in any form of expression—particularly in a great, evocative name that gives your DSI a head-start on contact. It's hard not to notice the DSI in these:

Diehard Batteries—The most dependable car batteries

The Airblade—The only blade-shaped, high-tech commercial hand dryer

Focus Factor—The pills that focus your memory

Destroyed in Seconds!—The reality show that shows great stuff blowing up

Princeton Longevity Center—The health clinic with check-ups that prolong your life

Seattle's Best Coffee—The coffee city's standard of excellence

Bare Naked Foods—The granola with the most natural, whole ingredients

Or it's Simply in the Performance

Not all products with a Dominant Selling Idea boast a great name or tagline. But every one *must* deliver great, consistent performance that proves the difference through tangible action if not words.

Volvo is the safe car. I've been saying it for years, but now, Volvo's become kind of newsworthy again because even though it hasn't advertised with a "safe" tagline for decades, in a recent survey, the century-old company was still named by 70% of consumers as *the world's safest car*. The Dominant Selling Idea is kept going by people and mechanics, who talk about the famous "steel safety cage." Or the fact that Volvo has unilaterally been responsible for nearly all the big personal safety inventions in cars since its inception—from the three-point seat belt to anti-lock brakes. And I just read they're keeping the legend alive by announcing a company-wide mission to build an injury-proof car by 2013. That's a 100-year-old heart that's still beating, folks.

Toyota by the same token is (embarrassing recalls of 2010 notwithstanding) "the car that doesn't break." Not a bad Dominant Selling Idea. I've never seen that in their tagline. I couldn't remember any of their taglines. But after polling all 17 of the Toyota owners I know and talking with my town's three local mechanics and hearing everyone lead with a version of the same idea—"they never come in for repairs," "They easily go 300,000 miles," "They don't break," "Only Honda's even come close in reliability," I've got the "best built, most durable" idea in my head and I happily pass it on to others (yes—those DSI laden words they tell me that I then pass along *are* consumer generated Micro-Scripts created by my friends and me, stimulated by performance and our direct experience—not from those company's taglines or marketing communications).

And Starbucks—the brand so many Gurus (used to) love to talk about, had neither a tagline nor advertising at all during its historic rise. The one whose DSI I'd describe as "the best coffee for aspiring people" created a warm coffeehouse atmosphere, European-style coffee selection, and then simply showed up in your neighborhood. On every street corner. In malls and book stores. They served consistently good coffee with a consistently comfortable place to sit for hours without you being asked to leave and get a job, and that was it.

Eventually, because it was also such expensive coffee (my friend calls it "Fourbucks"), they opened too many stores too quickly and started cutting corners on latte preparation, their DSI began to morph for a lot or people and their business began a historic dip.

A DSI in Every Product

And finally—we've been telling clients for years: if advertisers could have the chutzpah to brand bottled water, air, sand or marriage—there's a DSI in waiting in every company, product or service if you know where to look, no ifs, ands or buts. It takes no marketing budget, no national ad campaign, no nothing but some honest customer knowledge, belief in your product, and the courage to make the choice to pick yours. Some of the greatest in existence are found every day in small town USA. In my own little town, we have the Madison Art Cinema, Café Grounded—a coffee shop in an airplane hangar—and RJ Julia, who became America's preeminent independent bookseller.

The Five Ingredients of Your DSI

Five ingredients enable your proposition to be a Dominant Selling Idea. It tells people you are:

1. **"Best at."** It says you are number one at something— the <u>superlative</u> choice for a specific need. The best _____. The only one with _____. The most _____, etc.

2. **Important.** What you're #1 in has to be something that *matters*—something I really want or would want if I knew about it.

3. **Believable.** There has to be a unique, plausible *reason why* you claim the above that makes logical sense. It's nothing if it's not credible.

4. **Measurable.** It must be <u>specific</u> and obvious in your performance. It must be real in the walk, not just the talk; totally aligned and consistent with all your claims. Your performance must prove it.

5.   **Own-able.** Not already taken by somebody else. It must be uniquely available so you can stand for it.

Such an idea has the stuff to become the heart of the brand organism, and the foundation for effective Micro-Scripts that can succeed across any digital media.

Without a DSI at the heart, you end up with empty, engineless, self-serving communication with vague slogans like "A Passion for Excellence" or "You'll Notice the Difference—" or invisible, useless corporate names like *CQT Solutions.* These could be from anybody. The differentiating potential you get by using a DSI like "the 20,000-mile oil change" is rather obvious, isn't it?

Now let's go to the rules of thumb that govern the DSI.

These Are Your Seven DSI Rules of Thumb

1.   **We get <u>One</u> Item of Carry-on.**

If you're not yet convinced of this most important DSI rule, here are some other good reasons you should be. As humans, we have a love affair with the number one—with anything that comes in first, the leader, the best—and very little that comes after. That's why we famously can remember the tallest mountain in the world, the first man on the moon, our first kiss—but almost never the second. And third or fourth? Fuggedaboudit. We have one God and seek to be at one with ourselves. We reward winners out of all proportion to their talent over the second place finisher—even when they win by .0001 second as they often do in the Olympics.

We remember what we care about and we prove day in and day out that thing we care about is #1, literally and figuratively.

There are two DSI lessons here: if people love whatever is number one better than all else in the universe, then there is only one position in any category to claim that's worth a damn. We must be #1, the best, the gold medal winner in whatever category we inhabit. And if we're not, if someone else is already #1, we have to *invent a new category* to be the best in. We adjust our specialty. If there are already three regular dentists in town, become *the children's* dentist and you'll be instantly set apart. The other lesson is that if people are going to remember one thing—make sure it's a very special kind of idea. One with five ingredients...

2. **Test for Five Ingredients**

Test to see if it's a Dominant Selling Idea by checking off the five ingredients. It's only a DSI if it's:

1) **Best at.**

2) **Important.**

3) **Believable.**

4) **Measurable.**

5) **Own-able.**

3. **The Universal Paradox**

Even if people wanted long lists of features and benefits to remember instead of one all-important idea, it wouldn't work because a barrage of information—what most marketers throw at customers hoping something will stick—simply can't penetrate the human mind. Remember—our heuristic brains in times of stress or uncertainty want to discard information and shift to "one-reason decision making" to solve the most critical problems. Likewise, the heuristic brain gives us the **Universal Paradox** in all communications: The narrower you focus, the wider your message goes. The fewer things you say in each speech, the more you are heard. You get more general recognition by being the most specific. So those who can make the choice to pick a specialty to be best in—to "win the gold medal in"—are far more effective at achieving fame and recognition.

Being number one in safety like Volvo, brings with it reams of other positive associations. About quality construction, about superior technology, about corporate caring and responsibility and so on. This rule leads naturally to important corollaries.

4. Simple *Always* Wins

Simple beats difficult. Simple beats complicated. In practice and perception. Simple can be remembered, repeated, recommended and replicated. Simple means obvious. Simple means easy. Easy never lost to hard. The simple message wins.

5. Specific is Terrific

It's the difference between "low prices" and *Everything 50% Off!* The difference between "good athlete" and *High School All American.* Ivory is *99 and 44/100% pure.* As we'll see a little later—specificity is the metaphor writer's trick, the color added, the emotional trigger, the stuff of truth that supercharges ideas in the brain.

6. **The 3 Rs: Repeat, Repeat, Repeat**

There is no heart without repetition and reinforcement. That means for an idea to become a DSI, it has to be repeated not only by you but even more importantly—by others. You can't just force this as the brand police. They have to want to. Inside the organization your people have to understand, believe it, like it, be proud of it. Outside, it has to be important enough, easy enough and likeable enough for one customer to want to tell another and another.

The exact expression, especially peer-to-peer will vary, just like the telling of any joke or story. What holds it together is the spine.

7. *Other People's Heads* **are All that Counts**

By definition, a prospective DSI we create in strategic discussions is just a strategy. Then when we advertise it, it's just an *invitation* to outsiders to think of our product the way we'd like them to.

But to be a true working DSI, it has to be lodged in other people's heads or it's useless—a paper DSI. And the only way to accomplish that is through true, honest, uninflated performance. Ignore this reality of the Word of Mouth world at your peril. Some organizations go around assuming their Dominant Selling Idea is one thing, when even the simplest research would show they stand for a whole different experience in the consumer's mind. In fact, this can sometimes become your dominant *un-selling* idea, complete with consumer generated Micro-Scripts.

(I became leery of Nieman Marcus ever since I started hearing people jokingly call it "Needless Mark-up").

So, to establish a DSI in other people's heads, you can't just say it, you have to <u>do</u> it. Actually that would've been a great tagline for Dominant Selling Ideas: *Just Do It!*

I wonder if it's taken?

Last But Not Least: Making Dominant Selling Ideas into *Digital* Selling Ideas

As we optimize for the new master medium, Dominant Selling Ideas must function a little more like *Digital* Selling Ideas, a term I made up. It just means providing your Dominant Selling Idea with the Internet equipment it needs to play in digital traffic—while protecting the core identity that makes you a brand.

For example:

1. **We'll Have One DSI—But *Multiple* Micro-Scripts.** Brands traditionally sought one big Micro-Script to express the DSI—a TV tagline alone for example. Now we can use many, customized Micro-Scripts, optimized for different targets and channels. What's more, new Micro-Scripts will be dynamically generated by "the crowd" as they become emotionally invested in your product. Once the crowd gets the strategy, their genius kicks in. The brand keepers can't control it—but that's okay—they can mine it and steer it to keep to the Dominant Selling Idea. We give up a little control, to gain a lot more power.

2. **One Way—Becomes *Multi-way*.** Where marketing communication used to be a one direction process from broadcaster to captive listener—the new technology has made it forever a *multi-way* process. A hyper-conversation. The original message goes out from us. Consumers filter it and send it back to us and to their peers via their Word of Mouth Machines, very quickly, in a dizzying array, adding words or pieces to the message if they want while they go. The Digital Selling Idea operates in a perpetual feedback loop. A *responsiveness* loop. That means channels *in* become vital, not just the channels out.

Because of this new environment, the single heart of your story, the DSI is now more important than ever before. It must be virtually bulletproof. If you lose the idea heart, you've got brand nada in today's world.

Getting to the Digital Selling Idea will require providing the links, the social network connections, and all the other online tools that make it easy for you and your consumers to talk.

But, that said—listen to NO ONE who would try to convince you the medium *is* the message. The message will always be your promise of value, sharpened into a Dominant Selling Idea, riding into the mind in a properly-constructed Micro-Script.

Only the message can sell. Only the message can persuade.

The Internet, the social network sites or anything else—are channels.

Content is what this is all about, content as sharp as a knife. A differentiating idea at the center of any social media you build.

Pop Quiz

Okay, here's the end-of-chapter quiz. If this had been a presentation and I said, "so—what's one big takeaway that you could repeat tomorrow?" you'd say:

The DSI commandment. We have to find our heart, our...

A. Super Bowl commercial

B. Clever tagline

C. Really hot spokesmodel

D. Dominant Selling Idea

Since we're on the honor system, the answer is D.

Now onto the next section. For most organizations, finding and embracing a Dominant Selling Idea is a pretty big deal. You've got the heart of your brand, the ultimate defining difference in whatever it is you sell. Without it, it's nigh impossible to become a distinctive brand in this world. It's an idea around which employees can rally, customers can focus, and decisions can be guided. That puts you way ahead of most companies.

But in today's war room environment it's not enough.

To format your DSI to play in the mind, you'll need your Micro-Scripts...

Remember the Rules that Govern DSIs

I. The Official DSI Definition:

The DSI is your value proposition reduced to one ultimate advantage—the one item your customers would choose if they could choose just one.

It's what you're best at, that's important, believable, measurable, and own-able.

II. The DSI Rules of Thumb:

1. *The One Item of Carry-on Rule.*

2. *The Five Ingredients Rule:*
   "Best at," Important, Believable, Measurable, Own-able.

3. *The Universal Paradox:*
   Narrower and Sharper go Wider and Farther.

4. *Simple Always Wins.*

5. *Specific is Terrific.*

6. *The 3Rs: Repeat, Repeat, Repeat.*

7. *The Other People's Heads Rule.*

CHAPTER 6

What Goes into a Micro-Script?

The Micro-Script Equation

Now it gets interesting. Because we're going to look under the hood to see the moving parts, to get more of an understanding for devising our own magic words. Words that help our listeners to do things like "audiate—" that is, unconsciously complete our phrases in their heads before we even finish saying them. It's what happens when I say "If the glove doesn't fit…" *then I stop*—but your brain continues hearing *"you must acquit!"* Your brain "hears" the rest of the sentence as clearly as if I'd spoken it. Audiation is a term of music theory I learned recently from Donna Volpitta, a Ph.D. in childhood education who explained it's also the process babies use when learning to speak. Audiation helps them mimic and repeat the scripts they hear from their mothers until they've internalized the language. That's what Micro-Scripts do.

So scripting and repeating is natural to us from the very beginning. Micro-Scripts do it with metaphors, vivid imagery, rhythmic or rhyming cadences, brevity, and balanced logical constructions that make them the efficient little vehicles they are. They work so well because that's the way we learned language to begin with.

Now I want to assure any nervous students that this is not going to be tedious, overly technical or complex. I believe that like learning language, we shouldn't start with arcane rules or grammatical constructions. We learn best by hearing, seeing and saying until we start noticing and internalizing patterns.

And as in all things, practice makes perfect. Anyone who's fluent in the language has the capacity to create Micro-Scripts. I've seen fifth graders come up with great ones.

But whether or not you decide to derive them on your own or hire a team of talented copywriters (who these days are eager for your business)—understanding their basic construction is essential so you'll know 'em when you see 'em—so your objectives are clear and you can be most productive in guiding your team.

Learning By Example

Look at enough of these and you start seeing familiar structure and cadence.

Classic Clichés

Clichés are fun and helpful to start with because they represent some of the most effective Micro-Scripts of all time. A cliché is just a Micro-Script invented sometime in history that was so popular and true that it became a platitude. I say, so what if it's a cliché? Millions of people including you and me only know them because they're brilliant. A lot *were* invented by wise men like Ben Franklin, William Shakespeare and the writers of the Bible. Most are verbalized rules of thumb to cope with everyday living. Parents teach them to us to instill conventional wisdom. I find myself saying these to myself all the time…

Better safe than sorry.

If at first you don't succeed, try, try again.

Live and let live.

You only go around once.

No pain, no gain.

The squeaky wheel gets the grease.

What doesn't kill you makes you stronger.

The early bird gets the worm.

Honesty is the best policy.

Better late than never.

Life is too short for _____.

Hindsight is 20/20.

You snooze you lose.

Practice makes perfect.

There's no I in team.

Coulda, shoulda, woulda.

It's not whether you win or lose, it's how you play the game.

Beauty is as beauty does.

Let sleeping dogs lie.

Look before you leap.

If you can't beat 'em, join 'em.

Curiosity killed the cat.

Laughter is the best medicine.

When the going gets tough, the tough get going.

What goes around comes around.

...*And the golden rule*—a Micro-Script that some religious teachers believe sums up the Bible in one single sentence:

Do unto others as you'd have others do unto you.

One thing we just proved is that they are short and concise, indeed. Average length is about 5.2 words. But let's look at the patterns they reveal. Micro-Scripts are almost always constructed on one, or a combination of, the following four templates, together with a few key components.

Template 1. The A/B Equation

The pattern you'll see most often is a simple, two-part logic equation—a kind of balance where value A is related to value B to form a complete idea.

- **Problem A has Solution B**
- **If A, then B**
- **A causes B**
- **A vs. B**
- **A saves B**
- **A mirrors B**

And the single, big metaphor version:

A *is* B

For instance, A and B are underlined in the following:

<u>Honesty</u> is the best <u>policy</u>.   (A *is* B)

If <u>guns are outlawed</u>, only <u>outlaws</u> will
have <u>guns</u>.   (A mirrors B)

What <u>goes</u> around, <u>comes</u> around.   (If A, then B)

You <u>snooze</u> you <u>lose</u>.   (If A, then B)

No <u>pain</u>, no <u>gain</u>.   (A causes B)

Better <u>safe</u> than <u>sorry</u>.   (A saves B)

It's more subtle, but nonetheless present in others like:

What <u>doesn't kill</u> you makes you <u>stronger</u>. (A causes B)

If at first you <u>don't succeed</u>, <u>try</u>. . .   (Problem: A/
                                                            Solution: B)

<u>Look</u> *before you* <u>leap</u>.   (A saves B)

"Problem/solution" and "If/then" are the most fundamental selling tactics a junior copywriter is taught—or used to be taught anyway—when starting out at the ad agency. They're also the universal dynamics of the face-to-face sales interaction.

If persuasion means getting one person to change a value, to move mentally from one position to another, one can see that these Micro-Scripts are constructed to present a microcosm of that change—from one to another or truth to consequence.

A *is* B: The Single, Big Metaphor (Still Template 1)

The single, big metaphor Micro-Script where <u>A *is* B</u>, is one of the most universal and powerful of the A/B equations. When we are shown that "something is like something else," often in a new or startling way, we re-frame, re-align, re-think—we actually *hypnotize* ourselves with the new image.

In the clichés—virtually all contain metaphors that are at least implied. *Don't rock the boat* isn't about boating safety. The "boat" is a metaphor for any delicate situation in life that shouldn't be upset. Some more explicit A <u>*is*</u> B examples are:

Hindsight is 20/20.

Beauty is as beauty does.

Love is blind.

Laughter is (the best) medicine.

Again, some of history's greatest Micro-Scripts use the A *is* B equation. The domino theory: *Countries are dominos.* De Beers Diamonds: *A diamond is forever.*

Template 2. The Stark Reminder

The Stark Reminder doesn't waste time. It says: "Do or don't <u>do this</u>." It has a rhythm or word sequence that make us stand up and pay attention. From the clichés, we see examples like:

Never talk to strangers.

Practice makes perfect.

Life is too short for _____ .

Let sleeping dogs lie.

Live and let live.

And from modern Micro-Scripts, we'll see:

Just do it!

Stop, drop and roll (fire safety).

Keep on truckin'.

Save the whales.

Kill the bill!

Just say no!

Template 3. Unique Wordplay

The third most common pattern in Micro-Script construction is simply a unique, clever, entertaining word construction that lends itself to memory and speech. These almost always contain a rhyme or rhythm that appeals to the ear:

Woulda, coulda, shoulda.

MMMM mmmm good.

Snap, Crackle and Pop!

I came, I saw, I conquered.

Template 4. The Whole Micro-Story
(Nothing is more powerful)

Remember back in the Micro-Script definitions and Q&A when we said that a Micro-Script is *a story bite*—it either tells a story, or provides a story piece, or links to a story already running in the brain?

Well, some of the most amazing Micro-Scripts are built completely on their exposition of a whole story, more than rhythm, meter, an A/B equation or anything else. It's actually quite amazing how much of a story can be told in a sentence or less by an accomplished Micro-Script practitioner.

What Goes into a Micro-Script?

A colleague of mine gave me her favorite example—a little snippet she'd heard in a writing class a few years prior and could never forget.

For Sale: Baby Shoes. Never Worn.

Think about that for a minute. It's not a great rhyme or a word play. It's just story. Mysterious, provocative, crafty, fascinating.

Turns out there's more to this story in fact. According to legend, Ernest Hemingway wrote those words on a bet that he could tell a whole story in six words. This was his solution and supposedly, he thought it was one of the best stories he ever wrote.

Now it also turns out, as I've since discovered, there's a whole movement of folks, and websites and webzines which have spawned book compilations devoted to telling stories in six words or less—duplicating the challenge put to Ernest Hemingway in earnest.

Smith Magazine (www.smithmag.net) a blog/website dedicated to storytelling, launched a writing contest for "six-word memoirs"—entire life stories told in six words or less. That's a tall order. But they got enough responses to publish *Not Quite What I Was Planning*, a 200-page book of them. Here are a few six-word life stories I found just from flipping through the pages of that book:

Alaska hippie kid. Escaped via Ph.D. Melanie Brewer

Never should have bought that ring. Paul Bellows

Took scenic route. Got in late. Will Blythe

Study mathematics, marry slut. Sum bad. Dan Robinson

Found true love. Married someone else. Bjorn Stromberg

Being a monk stunk. Better gay. Bob Redman

Afraid of everything. Did it anyway. Ayse Erginer

The car accident changed my life. Kristin Stanefski

Atheist alcoholic gets sober through God. Bob Todd

Hard to write poems from prison. Ellen Goldstein

Detergent girl: Bold, Tide. Cheer. All. Martha Clarkson

Aspiring lady pirate, disillusioned, sells boat. Diana White

Long lost girl, recently found, unharmed. Tracy Bishop

After reading some of those marvelous six-worders, the point is obvious, don't you think? We prove yet again that we can say an amazing amount in six words. If you can describe a life in six words, or a novel or a movie, you've got to be able to make a communications point. You've got to be able to describe what your product or company does. The point of this book is that you must.

In that context, look again at the stories triggered by:

They're building a bridge to nowhere.

He ain't heavy, he's my brother.

Or from some of the greatest ad copywriting in history:

They laughed when I sat down at the piano, but when I started to play... considered by many the greatest headline ever written. And others like:

Always a bridesmaid but never a bride.

Only her hairdresser knows for sure.

The man in the Hathaway shirt[*]

The people who write TV and movie titles are some of the best in the world at creating story-imbued Micro-Scripts for those titles. Maybe it's because they're professional storytellers. The point is, you can get an amazing amount of information and story suggestion in memorable titles like:

Raise the Titanic!

Desperate Housewives

Texas Chainsaw Massacre

---

[*] He was the dapper guy with the eye patch in the ads a few years ago—a combination *visual* Micro-Script and verbal. The visual said there's something exotic and romantic about this guy. He probably just had a bad case of conjunctivitis but who's asking? He made Hathaway the #1 dress shirt brand for men for decades.

and of course that favorite of millions:

Beverly Hills Grandma: Profile of a Hooker

Don't ever forget the locomotive power of story on the human brain. A great marketer once said, "You can make a speech on an important subject for two hours, and fifteen minutes later, your audience has forgotten the whole thing. But tell someone a story. And twenty years later they'll come back and repeat it to you word for word." And that's why story is one of the greatest tools for creating powerful Micro-Scripts. And Micro-Scripts are the greatest tools for compressing powerful stories into cell phone screen-sized packages—just right for communicating in our hyper-connected world.

Combinations

Very few Micro-Scripts are 100% one template or the other. Combinations are the norm. For example, in just four words, *You snooze you lose* has 1) A/B Equation, and 2) a Stark Reminder. It also contains some key ingredients—Rhyme, Alliteration and a Repetitive Sequence—special components we'll talk about next.

Key Ingredients:
1. Word Patterns, Rhythms and Rhymes

It should be obvious by now that Mrs. Goodworthy, your eighth grade English teacher who was trying so hard to teach you the mechanics of poetry—rhyming structure, alliteration, consonance, assonance and repetitive word sequences—while you sat there bored—was merely trying to show you how to make millions of dollars or get elected to high office by mastering the phonetic secrets of Micro-Scripts.

Rhymes, rhythms and such are key components that make Micro-Scripts say-able, play-able, like-able, stick-able and just plain interesting. Here are some others mixed in with the clichés:

When in <u>doubt</u>, throw it <u>out</u>.	Simple Rhyme
No <u>pain</u>, no <u>gain</u>.	Simple Rhyme
<u>Practice</u> makes <u>perfect</u>.	Alliteration
An apple <u>a day</u> keeps the doctor <u>away</u>.	Complex Rhyme
<u>Don't</u> ask, <u>don't</u> tell.	Repetitive Sequence
Think <u>globally</u>, act <u>locally</u>.	Assonance, Complex Rhyme
When the <u>going gets tough</u>, the <u>tough get going</u>.	Complex Repetitive Sequence
<u>Quicker</u>, <u>thicker</u>, <u>picker-upper</u>.	Complex Rhyme
<u>Curiosity</u> <u>killed</u> the <u>cat</u>.	Alliteration
<u>Click it</u> or <u>ticket</u>.	Complex Rhyme
<u>Stop</u>, <u>drop</u> and <u>roll</u>.	Rhyme and Assonance
The family that <u>prays together</u>, <u>stays together</u>.	Rhyme, Assonance, Repetitive Sequence

But even when a big rhyme or matching vowels isn't obvious, there's virtually always strong *meter*—a cadence or a simple beat like a drum that helps it out. Imagine beating a drum as you say these:

> *Don't rock the boat.* (Say: Bmp, bmp, *ba*-BMP)
>
> *No place like home.*
>
> *The early bird gets the worm.*
>
> *Buy low, sell high!*

2. Vivid, Colorful Language

Birds, worms, boats, cats, shoulda, snooze, squeaky wheels, pain, apples and doctors—good Micro-Scripts employ colorful, strong, evocative words whenever they can. Even in the clichés which are rather old and dowdy compared to a lot of what's new, this type of language is preferred by successful Micro-Script makers.

We want words that show, not tell. That's why words like *passion, quality, commitment, dedication, excellence, difference,* and *deliver* find their way into lots of corporate mission statements—but not into Micro-Scripts. In fact, most employees (including senior management) couldn't repeat the company mission statement if they tried.

Just don't forget—your <u>number one priority</u> in a Micro-Script is the sum total of the idea or the value you're putting forth—not language for its own sake. It's the wisdom plus a bit of rhythmic phrasing that makes *What goes around comes around,* and *Practice makes perfect* timeless and universal, not anything colorful in their individual words.

3. Simple Metaphors

By now you know this is last but definitely not least when it comes to Micro-Scripting. Metaphors not only make the audience color your premise with their own individual experience—they almost automatically assure you of using vivid, colorful language when you're creating a Micro-Script. They have to be specific, concrete, physical, almost tactile to do their work.

Life is like a box of chocolates.

An infinitely large and mysterious thing is like the littlest, most specific and familiar thing. A box of chocolates. I can taste it, I can smell it, and I can remember all the times I bit into one as a little kid and didn't know what I was gonna get. (So I ate the whole box).

Finally—There's A DSI in Every One

Remember the third Big Rule? A marketing Micro-Script must be built on a Dominant Selling Idea? Well, even in the old clichés, there's a lesson, a moral, a value or a central idea implicit in every one. Without a point of view, a Micro-Script has no worth to anyone, and it won't be passed along.

No pain, no gain:	DSI: Achievement is earned.
We only go around once:	DSI: Don't waste opportunity.
What doesn't kill you	DSI: Adversity builds

makes you stronger:	character.
Look before you leap:	DSI: Beware of foolish impulses.
If at first you don't succeed, try, try again:	DSI: Don't be a quitter.
Beauty is as beauty does:	DSI: It's what's inside that counts.
Bridge to nowhere:	DSI: Government spending is wasteful and corrupt.

So Let's Sum It Up

Even the oldest, some say tired-est (but not me, I love 'em) Micro-Scripts have consistent constructions that include either the A/B Equation, the Stark Reminder, the Unique Wordplay, a whole Micro-Story, or all four.

They employ word patterns, rhythms, rhymes and/or distinctive meter, and colorful word choices—and they always contain a key idea or value at the center.

Now let's see if the patterns continue in the more modern Micro-Scripts.

Social Micro-Scripts/Modern Lessons

Some of the following are so famous, they probably also have a little cliché DNA, but they're hip nonetheless. We use them for conventional wisdom, to flavor speech, influence behavior, and win arguments.

> The _____ (boyfriend, mother-in-law, dog, dentist) from hell.

> _____ (boyfriends, mother-in-laws, dogs, dentists) are people too!

> Hate is not a family value.

> The family that prays together, stays together.

> Only YOU can prevent forest fires.

> Don't be a litterbug.

> What would Jesus do?

> Black is beautiful.

> You are what you eat.

> Think outside the box.

> If you're not part of the solution, you're part of the problem.

> He's just not that into you.

> A moment on the lips, a lifetime on the hips.

> Be kind, rewind.

Okay, what patterns do we see? Again it's rare that any popular script runs over six words. That's not a hard stop, just a benchmark. Most are metaphor-based.

Incidentally—*What would Jesus do* implies metaphorically "You are Jesus."

Rhythmic patterns and sequences are obvious in ones like *stays together, prays together, part of the solution, part of the problem, lips and hips,* etc.

Speaking of lips—one of the greatest, most effective Micro-Scripts of all times came from World War II, to remind citizens to keep secrets, secret:

Loose lips sink ships.

Politics

We've certainly covered this genre by this point. But for your convenience, I've re-listed some of the great ones so you can review them from an anatomy standpoint. Again, I love that observation: "a political campaign is a one-day sale for 100% market share." Campaigns hire some of the most ambitious and creative minds out there to deliver that one-day sale. And once the election is won, many Micro-Script makers stay on and use their skills to communicate on policy and issues. This group has truly contributed some of most impactful Micro-Scripts in history to the public domain.

Evocative, colorful metaphors are one of their hallmarks:

The flip-flopper.

Countries like dominos.

Bridges to nowhere.

Death tax.

Read my lips, no new taxes (there's those lips again).

The silent majority.

The moral majority.

The war on terror.

Death panels, pull the plug on grandma (in the health reform debate).

...to name a few.

Marketing, Selling and Branding

As I've mentioned, advertising writers used to be really, really good at this. They created the language for mass-market selling that everybody used when it came to the great brands—usually memorialized in taglines that became part of the American lexicon. This was true especially during the heyday of advertising—what some have called the American century.

Why don't we see scripts as clever and succinct as *Melts in your mouth, not in your hand,* or *Good to the last drop* anymore?

Well, in fact we do—when marketing people remember that their job is to sell and put people in motion, rather than solely to amuse people and get noticed for entertainment which has nothing to do with why they're getting paid.

The ones who aren't fooling around—the ones who have a candidate to sell *or else,* or who understand that going viral with a Dominant Selling Idea attached vs. just going viral can be the difference between moving markets or just moving email—they will be the business winners. You have a choice.

You get to choose whether you have a *Made from sugar so it tastes like sugar, Shoes that breathe* or *Vestas, No. 1 in modern energy*, vs. a generic slogan like *Now that's eating*. I can remember that line only because I thought it was so bad. Sitting here without looking back at my notes, I can't tell you which pizza chain it represented. I can tell you though, that when I'm scarfing down a Twinkie, I also think that's eating.

Here's a representative sample of some of the great ones, again for convenient placement during our anatomy lesson. Look at all the patterns and components that keep many of these working perfectly after twenty, thirty, eighty years.

Tastes great, less filling.

A mind is a terrible thing to waste.

I'm going to Disney World!

I shoulda had a V-8.

The few, the proud, the Marines.

Join the Navy and see the world.

Fair and balanced news.

Guinness is good for you!

You deserve a break today.

What Goes into a Micro-Script?

Carnival are the FUN ships.

Fly the friendly skies.

Softens hands while you do dishes.

Got milk?

Pork is the other white meat.

Nothing gets between me and my Calvins.

Snap, Crackle and Pop!

It's good to the last drop.

Crest is the one dentists recommend.

Wheaties...

M&Ms...

Allstate...

Micro-Scripts for Teaching and Instruction

Lastly I want to mention another crucial application—Micro-Scripts for invented rules of thumb. When we face situations that are dangerous, difficult or dire—high-speed situations in particular—we've learned to go to, what else—verbalized heuristics in the fastest, surest, clearest, easiest to remember format. It begins with an M.

When we make them up, we use our templates and our key components—just like any great Micro-Script.

Take landing a jet.

When you're landing, there's a set of runway lights on the side that tell you if you're high, low or on the safe glide path. With a dozen other factors to monitor in the final seconds, pilots need a fast, fail-safe rule of thumb to remind them what the light code means without consulting a manual. Two white lights, one over the other, means you're high. Two red means you're low. Now logically, the safe glide slope should be in between—white over red, right? But it's the opposite—*it's red over white* because of the machine's optics. Needless to say, you can't afford to forget this fact, even once. So the pilots use a Micro-Script:

Red over white, you're all right. Red over red, you're dead.

I've used it and it works.

Or take sailing on a windy day.

In a small boat, a big gust can capsize you in seconds. Or sometimes when it's really blowing, things just start getting out of hand. The proper action is to let out the sails immediately. It's kind of like stepping on the brake in your car.

The Micro-Script you're taught in sailing school is:

When in doubt, let it out.

When bringing a boat into a tight channel, if the helmsman forgets what side of the buoy to stay on, the boat hits the rocks. Heading into the harbor, red buoys are always on the right side of the channel, green on the left.

What Goes into a Micro-Script?

So the famous Micro-Script is:

Red, right, returning.

I've been going in and out of harbors for forty years and I swear, I repeat that Micro-Scripted rule of thumb in my head every single time.

We have them for driving—*steer in the direction of the skid.* We have them for sports, work, or in my case, spelling. I can't spell the word "recieve" unless I say to myself: "*I before E except after C.*" See, it was supposed to be Rec<u>ei</u>ve.

Here's one final one that everybody in the world seems to know. A nautical/meteorological one:

Red sky at morning, sailors take warning.
Red sky at night, sailors delight.

It's such a nifty little phrase, people say it and repeat it all around the world, especially when they're down near the coast at sunset.

But I don't think anyone in the world ever had a clue what it meant.

Now we'll spend a little time on the art and science of crafting Micro-Scripts, vetting them and maintaining them.

Remember What Micro-Scripts are Made Of

1. The Four Templates:
   - i) A/B Equation:
     - Problem A has Solution B
     - If A, then B
     - A causes B
     - A vs. B
     - A saves B
     - A *is* B
     - A mirrors B
   - ii) The Stark Reminder
   - iii) Unique Wordplay
   - iv) A Whole Micro-Story

2. Key Ingredients
   - Word Patterns, Rhythms and Rhymes
   - Vivid, Colorful Language
   - Simple Metaphors

3. There must be a DSI—an idea, a moral or a theme inside.

CHAPTER 7

Create Your Own

—"What's an iPod? It's 10,000 songs in your pocket."

Author's Note

At the time of this writing, after speaking on the subject of Micro-Scripts on three continents, talking about it on the radio, even writing an Op Ed for *The Boston Globe* on political Micro-Scripts during the great health care debate, people seem to agree on two things: 1) The Micro-Script rules are both sagacious and real, and, 2) They want *theirs*.

What my colleagues and I still needed to agree on was describing the best process for doing it—especially if you're not a professional copywriter or speechwriter which means 99% of everyone. How do you just come up with awesome little gems like the iPod "10,000 songs" metaphor above?

The simplest answer: by combining a mix of passion about your subject, a desire to focus, a willingness to experiment, and a commitment to listen to what others are **repeating,** after they've heard it.

But you need more than platitudes at this point. You need a conscious method to jump-start your process. So, like a pro golfer trying to explain how he swings a golf club without thinking—we decided to deconstruct what we've been doing for decades. I stopped writing this manuscript for a few months to literally watch our own process, discuss it with other communicators, and test it out.

What follows are a short set of practical steps that can produce a solid set of Micro-Scripts for just about anyone. And I must say—after going through this little bit of self-examination and understanding it ourselves, we are getting to the bottom line in our own branding work faster, smarter and simpler than ever during the last twenty-five years. For me, the old adage is really true: "We learn most when we endeavor to teach."

Quick Check of Our Dominant Selling Idea

Skydivers do a "pin check" just before they jump to make sure the parachute is clear and ready. Micro-Scripters do a DSI check to make sure their big idea is clear and ready because it's the actual heart of the matter itself.

By now you know that the Dominant Selling Idea is simply the big, differentiating idea you want to get across and have people pass along to others. The primary value you stand for. The one item of mental "carry-on" you want others to take aboard.

In other words, it is **what** you want your Micro-Script to express in an arresting, repeatable way.

This big, central idea has been called all kinds of things in marketing history—from the USP (Unique Selling Proposition), to Positioning, to Brand Essence in some cases.

But it's not just for brands and corporate identities. It's the key point you're making on *any* subject of importance. It's the crux of the answer that piques a buyer's interest or erases a buyer's objection with irresistible, convincing, proof.

Bottom line, your Micro-Script has to be **about something specific.** You need to know what that is and be able to explain it enough beforehand to turn it into a sharp little Micro-Script like *10,000 songs in your pocket.* For example—

- You're the first synthetic fiber that's warmer than down, or
- You're the German car that has the best engineering, or
- You're the safest tire, or
- Guaranteed lowest price, or
- You're the one with the character to stick to your political principles while your rudderless opponent's values shift back and forth with the political winds.

These descriptions of unique values or attributes aren't Micro-Scripts yet, they are the Dominant Selling Ideas that stake out your competitive advantage. In the German car example, the legendary Micro-Script turned into *the ultimate driving machine.* The politician's un-anchored opponent became *the flip-flopper.* But to come up with such great verbalizations, someone had to know and state their DSI beforehand.

So We Don't Start at Square One, We Start at Square Two

We start where the vast majority of us find ourselves when trying to tell someone the big difference about our business.

That is, we're pretty sure of the main idea we stand for, but haven't exactly made it crystal clear in a definitive way, either to ourselves or to our employees. If we asked ten associates the same question, we'd get ten different answers. We're not that good at summarizing it in less than a minute.

The discovery process we'll use to come up with Micro-Script material has the added benefit of sharpening our sense of our own big idea as we go. You'll come out with a more solid definition of your DSI *and* the Micro-Scripts to help verbalize it. Two birds with one stone.

Seriously now, if you really *are* starting at Square One, undecided about what your basic Dominant Selling Idea is or needs to be:

1) Go back and read Chapter 5; 2) If you need even more details, get a copy of *Why Johnny Can't Brand: Rediscovering the Lost Art of the Big Idea;* or pick up a copy of the legendary *Positioning: The Battle for Your Mind* by Al Ries and Jack Trout, or; 3) Hire a professional positioning firm to figure it out with you. It's never going to be a Micro-Script without the idea.

Here's The Process
Hypothesize,
>Plagiarize,
>>Memorialize,
>>>Synthesize

Okay, I just made up that rhyming headline but it really does cover it.

In the **hypothesize** and **plagiarize** stages we'll gather up all our raw materials, we'll pan for Micro-Script gold—mainly by asking <u>lots of questions</u>. We say the word "plagiarize" lovingly. It really means borrowing best practices from the masters.

In the **memorialize** stage, we'll actually take our gathered gold and write out a very short, no more than one page narrative. This can be either what we call a "brand story," a short speech, or a piece of sample ad copy. I'll explain later why this is such a crucial step, but it's no accident that so many Micro-Scripts are born in the midst of political speeches, articles by journalists and copy from ad writers. The physical process of writing it out puts the brain in story and metaphor mode and warms it up for Micro-Scripts, whether you're a writer by trade or not.

In the **synthesize** stage, we take the best phrases and language threads from our story and peel them off into an initial set of Micro-Scripts we can launch in the market.

From then on we use our ears and eyes—we listen, we observe, and we converse with our audience to see what gets *re-prised* (repeated), and which ones to *re-vise*—or discard altogether.

I'll lay the process out, then I'll illustrate with examples of the process in action in the real world.

Finding Your Raw Material—Panning for Gold

As any experienced brand consultant, communicator, salesperson or screenwriter will tell you, your best material comes <u>90% from asking and listening</u> and only about 10% from assembly. Generating Micro-Scripts, especially your first set of them, is no exception.

1. Hypothesize—Pose Some Simple Questions

This part is so basic, yet it's the key. You're going to ask people inside and outside your organization to *tell you* all about your big idea. Success is a matter of asking questions until the other person inevitably puts the answers in the palm of your hand, or as those of us in sales like to say, "they give you the keys to the safe." You're going out with a note pad to have a conversation about your subject. You want their stories, their metaphors, their experiences and their descriptions in their words through their filters. It's very similar to the research and discovery process you'd go through to find your Dominant Selling Idea in the first place, but now you're really listening hard for stories and language.

Who Should You Talk To?

Your stakeholders, top to bottom. And I'm not exaggerating—the lowest on the ladder can be more prescient sometimes than the most senior executive. Remember—"Out of the mouths of babes..."

So if it's for a business, talk to employees from the mail room up to the management floor, to actual customers, prospects, people who saw your product but didn't buy, competitors' employees or former-employees and maybe an analyst or two. Reserve a special time slot for salespeople—they're the ones already putting your idea into words each day and living by them.

People will tell you amazing, illuminating things about what needs to be sold, told and how to tell it. They'll articulate in all kinds of ways what your big idea *really is*—what they and others think you stand for—the direct, physical result of their experiences with your product and company. They'll tell you about your competitor's strengths and vulnerabilities. They will provide you with vivid selling language, colorful metaphors and examples, all kinds of creative material, for *free*.

When you go through this step, I promise...

- You will ALWAYS be surprised by something.
- You will be amazed at the likelihood that someone you never expected, without realizing it, simply lays a great Micro-Script idea in your lap. Sometimes, you'll even walk away with a killer tagline or a new name that somebody just hands you.

What Will You Ask Them?

You'll ask them to have a conversation with you about the big idea you're looking to crystallize and verbalize. You'll always ask "open questions"—what sales trainers used to call the "six honest serving men" that elicit thoughtful replies vs. a yes or no:

> "I have six honest serving men, they tell me all I know.
> There names are **what** and **why** and **who** and **when**
> and **where** and **how**."

Ask, even if you think you know the answers beforehand. I promise, there are some you don't.

Here's an example of a dozen questions we might ask people when we're exploring a big idea for a company's brand positioning. We ask, what is it? Why is it? How is it? And *what if...*

1. **What part of the industry do you specialize in and what customers do you serve? Are you the leader?**

2. Does this specialty have a common name?

3. Why does the world need your company?

4. What do you do for people that nobody else does? How important is it to your customers? Do you stand for that *by name* in your customers' minds? Does anybody?

5. Who are your competitors? What are they famous for?

6. What's your "unsung" ability—the#1 thing the market needs to know about your company they don't know now?

7. How do you say your value proposition: (Fill in the blanks): "We're the #1 choice for, (or) we're the best at _____ . That's because we have

   _____ .

8. If we asked five customers, what would *they* say your company stands for?

9. What if we said this _____ (or this) is your big difference. What you're going stand for. Would it be true? Would people believe it? Would they be excited by it? Why or why not?

10. What keeps you up at night about the company?

11. What makes you most proud?

Create Your Own

12. **Against your toughest competition, why will you win and what could make you lose in the future?**

You're using your questions to facilitate a *conversation;* it's not an interrogation or a news conference. When you hear something interesting, go ahead, veer away from your formal set of questions. Just keep using the six honest serving men (what, why, who, when, where, how) until you hit pay dirt.

You never know where it's going to lead…

> Q: Okay, so you're #1 in "environmentally friendly house paints." That's great.
> Now, *what* keeps you up at night?
> A: Thinking about what the trade press will do when they discover our secret formula.
>
> Q: And *how* will you be affected by that?
> A: Well, our respected family tradition might be affected, especially in our line of *Eco-Green Earth Lover* paints.
>
> Q: And *why* do you lose sleep over that?
> A: Well, we still add a tiny smidgen of lead.
>
> Q: Hmmmnnn. And *what* do you mean by a tiny smidgen?
> A: 85%.
>
> Q: I see. And *why* are you concerned about that?
> A: Because they won't look at all the good we do as a company. The little league team we sponsor or the talent show. They'll only look at the 30% *who get poisoned.*

> Q: So, *what* should the market know you *really* stand for?
>
> A: How bout, *Old Fashioned* <u>*Paint Flavor*</u>?

No Right Answers, Just Right Questions

The questions you ask obviously reflect the issue, the product, the context and the person you're speaking to. When you get into the conversation, you'll make them up on the fly. The iPod example of *10,000 songs in your pocket* was an original tagline in the early ads. Actually, it started as *1,000 songs in your pocket*. Where could it have come from? A question like this in a conversation: Q: *"What comes into your mind when you think of that little device in your pocket?"*

A: *"I go wow, I've got a thousand songs in there. <u>A thousand songs in my pocket!</u>"*

The great ones can happen just like that—you just have to be listening for them.

Some Real World Examples of Golden Nugget Mining

Keep listening and you will find some 18kt. gold.

This next one was given to me in our seventeenth interview at a global insurance brokerage firm. A district manager said:

"I was trained as a CPA. I look at risk like any other financial component because by definition, to be in business, all companies assume risk. My clients are ships on this sea of risk—the better I help them navigate, the more they save, the more liability they avoid, the more competitive advantage they have. That's a very positive thing. The whole world just thinks of risk as negative, as mitigating loss. I think of risk as a *positive opportunity*—a leverage-able quantity to manage for financial gain. It's a big difference from the traditional thinking. And if we can show them we have the world's best data to back it up, they'll believe us."

Indeed it was a big difference. The idea that one company could actually *"re-position" risk from negative to positive* by disrupting the industry standard vision, backed by proprietary technology, gave this multi-billion dollar insurance firm a clearer articulation of its Dominant Selling Idea along with the Micro-Script:

They give you a *Return on Risk.*[7]

Stay tuned because in the case studies coming up, there'll be more real examples to show how casual responses to your questions turn into Micro-Scripts.

2. Plagiarize—Borrow the Already Proven from the Already Great Who are Already Around You

In Chapter 3, I told you about Don Moine, the famous sales-scripting pioneer who was paid hundreds of thousands of dollars by large companies to do one thing: To follow the company's sales superstars around and transcribe the exact wording they would use when approaching a prospect, presenting key points, answering objections, and closing the sale.

Don's academic research showed him that these super-stars—the top 1% of that famous top 20% who do all the selling—the ones who sold a hundred times more than their colleagues—possessed a natural, probably unconscious ability along with good work habits. They used a kind of *mesmerizing speech*, mostly because they told a lot of stories and metaphors.

They painted word pictures with vivid language. In short, they were naturally using Micro-Script language.

So sales managers didn't need to guess or make anything up. They just had to take out a note pad and jot down the Micro-Scripts these folks with a natural talent were already saying, then put them into what he called a Mastermind script book for all the rest of the sales force to repeat for themselves. Don claimed that in some organizations, sales jumped 40–50% within weeks of unleashing these books on the sales force. And some companies found them so valuable, they would number each one, collect them at the end of the day and lock them up so competitors couldn't steal their magic words.

Our point here is simple: There is probably no more juicy, low-hanging Micro-Script fruit for you to pluck, fully formed and proven, than the ones already used by the best people who sell your product or others like it.

I hear them telling me Micro-Scripts everywhere I go:

> Every time a real professional closes me on
> another sale…

Over the holidays I walked into our local action sports store to buy a winter jacket called a *Down Sweater* by Patagonia, the great outdoor clothing company. I was there for a Down Sweater and a Down Sweater only, because this stranger at another store had already told me about it. The guy was so proud of his own jacket, he introduced himself and said, "I couldn't help overhearing that you're looking for a good jacket: here, try this on." He took the jacket off his back and handed it to me. He said, "Isn't it light? Isn't it warm? It's the best jacket I've ever owned. It's all I wear. It's the Down Sweater from Patagonia!"

Needless to say, I was floored by this incredible Word of Mouth fireworks display, captured in the wild. I determined I was going get one for Christmas and kept on thinking about it for three straight days until I finally had time to get to my local Trail Blazer store. I walked in a committed brand buyer, loaded for Down.

I walked up to Kevin the floor assistant and said, "Do you have a Down Sweater by Patagonia?" And that's when I heard the Micro-Scripts.

He replied: "It's a great item and we have it. But it's not THE jacket. For the same price, try *the one I just bought for myself*. The Arc'teryx Atom." He said:

1. "This is *lighter and warmer because its made of* Coreloft *their newest synthetic fiber*.

2. Unlike Down, *Coreloft* stays warm even when it's wet. *But here's the amazing thing:*

3. Coreloft actually *transfers the heat around inside the jacket* from the warmer parts to the colder parts *to evenly warm up your body:*

   wanna see it, I'll prove it to you."

Kevin then ran into the back and came out a minute later with this square of white material that looked like fiberglass insulation. "Hold out both palms," he said.

4. "Feel you palm getting hot? It actually <u>stores the heat</u> <u>from your body</u>. Now flip it over onto your other palm. Feel the heat immediately? It's transferring!

5. It's <u>like wearing an electric mitten!</u>"

Wow, I said, I can feel it. He said, you can buy the Down Sweater. But THIS is the jacket!

I bought two. One for my wife and one for me. I wear it to bed I like it so much. I wear it in the shower.

So what just happened here?

Kevin was a superstar salesperson. He had a complete Micro-Pitch (Micro-Scripts strung together into a complete elevator pitch) all ready for me that was so quick and convincing, it was irresistible.

Why did I know they were Micro-Scripts? Because I went home and I repeated them to the whole family three times during the gift exchange on Christmas Eve, that's why. I transferred the pitch via Word of Mouth using Kevin's content. I **plagiarized**. I said "Honey: I was walking in to Trail Blazer, all sold on the Down Sweater. Until I tried out THE jacket. The *one the guy at Trail Blazer owns. It's made of Coreloft, their newest synthetic fiber. It not only keeps you warm when its wet, it transfers the heat around inside the coat to evenly warm up your body. Like wearing an electric mitten!* It's amazing. *Down can't do that!* He put a sample of the Coreloft stuff in my hands to prove it!"

If I was the wholesale rep for Arc'teryx, I'd put those six little scripts on a piece of paper, hand them to every store manager in my territory, and watch them sell jackets.

In other words, I'd plagiarize the words of a mesmerizing Micro-Pitch given by a top salesperson, and sell happily ever after.

You see, you don't have to invent great Micro-Scripts if you just listen and pass them on. So don't let great Micro-Scripts *evade-your-eyes*. Remember to *Plagiarize!*[8]

It'll be one of your greatest sources of Micro-Script material.

Hear George Clooney Use Sales Micro-Scripts

Have you seen the movie *Up in the Air* with George Clooney? He plays a hired gun corporate hatchet man. Sitting across from each new fire-ee, he has a Micro-Script he uses to deflect the shock in the execution room. He tells them they should thank the company:

> *The fact is every person who ever did something great in this world, who fulfilled their destiny or built an empire, had to first sit in that chair and hear these words from someone like me. It's a wake-up call to follow your dreams.*

It actually helped some. And it established the control position for George Clooney vs. the numb and dumbfounded.

How do I know it's a Micro-Script? Because he said it to virtually every person in the movie he fired. His arrogant little colleague-in-training copied it the minute she got in trouble with a candidate, and used it faithfully thereafter. I remembered it too, and just wrote it here. George Clooney was the top 1% road warrior at his firm, the man with the mesmerizing language patterns. He might have plagiarized these magic words from another mentor. Who cares? You make up some, you mimic some, you deploy the ones that work.

You'll find great words to borrow for every part of the sales and communications process, starting with the initial approach.

I've used the Dale Carnegie greatest approach script in all kinds of situations since I first heard it. It's the opening that <u>has</u> to elicit either one of two responses: "Yes," or "what is it?"

> *If there was a way to [insert key claim] (cut your sales costs by 50% and double your revenues), you'd want to know about it, wouldn't you?*

That opening has been taught to tens of thousands of salespeople, instantly opening millions of prospects to new propositions, no matter how busy, disinterested or even hostile they might initially be.

It's a brilliant Micro-Script that Dale Carnegie provided for every student to share. It's so simple. I'm glad they thought of it.

Summary of Tips on How To Mine the Masters

1. Ask the best salespeople you know to tell you. Listen to their stories and solutions.

2. Follow your superstars on sales calls and note word for word how they deal with every situation.

3. Watch and listen at conferences.

4. Note the most compelling words and phrases in your industry's best ads.

3. Memorialize—Jot Down a Little Story; Let the Story Crystallize More Ideas

"The best headline's always <u>in the copy</u>."

Journalists and advertising writers learn on day one that there's nothing more important or challenging to write than a great headline. In a sentence or less, sometimes a couple of words, the headline has to stop a busy consumer, attract, spark interest and suggest a promise, all at the same time. Or else the page gets flipped, the copy never gets read or the magazine never gets bought. That's a lot of work for five or six words. Indeed, while not all headlines qualify as Micro-Scripts unless they are actually repeated by consumers, they must always be story bites. They've got the same DNA as any Micro-Script.

Any great tagline too, is in this same special bucket. In a sense, it's your brand's permanent headline, so it's really important to get it right. One of the best techniques you can ever learn to get it right is by simply putting together a little story, and coming up with it as you write out the sentences.

Let me explain:

I was a junior copywriter at the legendary advertising agency that wrote the book on creating great headlines and taglines—a place called Ted Bates in New York.

Bates invented a concept called the USP (Unique Selling Proposition)* and employed it to create Micro-Scripted tagline

---

* USP was the Ted Bates term for the one big differentiating idea that every brand must have to set itself apart in a crowded marketplace. It's the foundation of what we later updated, expanded a bit, and renamed the Dominant Selling Idea.

gems that resonated for decades like *Melts in your mouth, not in your hand*, *Rolaids spells R-E-L-I-E-F*, *Wonder Bread builds strong bodies twelve ways*, *Hefty bags are tough enough to overstuff* and *Halls has vapor action.* Our creative director actually wrote *Get a piece of the rock* for Prudential, a breakthrough phrase to put on an insurance company in those days. They invented, amazingly, terms like *acid indigestion.*

Bate's own tagline was: *Think globally, act locally,* a classic Micro-Script. But their Dominant Selling Idea was always simply, "The USP Agency."

Soon after I got there, my boss told me a little copywriter's secret for writing headlines and taglines that turns out to be just as relevant for creating Micro-Scripts, since they share so many attributes.

Of course he told it to me in a seven-word Micro-Script that I never forgot:

The best headline's always in the copy.

Here's what he meant and here's why it's important to us:

Advertising writers invariably start writing an ad by coming up with the headline first. Because as I said above, they know the headline probably needs to do 85% of the work in any ad since 85% of the audience will probably never read the copy. The headline is the spine of the ad from which all else grows.

At Ted Bates, though, there was a step even before writing any part of the ad: we were required to write the USP tagline for the whole campaign first, before we were ever allowed to write headlines or copy. We were taught that there had to be a central, strategic selling idea before anything else—an idea that would focus all the headlines, the ads, and the creative long after any single ad. The big idea was paramount at Bates, not anybody's clever ad execution.

So we'd think of the central selling idea and come up with taglines in a vacuum without visuals or graphics. Some would be pretty good. *Then* we'd write the headlines and copy for the ad.

And here's what happened nearly every time—

The creative director would read the copy, and underline a buried phrase or two in it and say, "*here's* your headline or your tagline. Put that at the top now and see how much better this is." And it always was.

Because the process of writing the body copy was the same as telling a story. A problem, a solution, a little bit of drama in the context of everyday life for those in need of the answer that only your product can provide. The mental process of writing out any story activates the mind to think in metaphors, scenarios, examples, vivid words and word pictures. It warms up the brain's expressive machinery. And out come those nuggets, this time from your keypad—the gems that are interesting, memorable, powerful, compelling, succinct, relatable and very likely, repeatable too.

Think of your mind as a plane needing a runway to get flying. It takes about a mile or so to gain speed for lift off. For Micro-Script makers, that runway is the story you start writing from all the interviews and notes you've got, from the language you've plagiarized, and from your own natural synthesis that comes with concentrating on any idea for a little time. You start writing. One sentence, two sentences, three...and you're... airborne. You're in the story zone—a mesmerizing place. Ideas and language start coming and coalescing. It really works.

I'll tell you that to this day, when I see ads from most copywriters—even experienced ones, I spot what ought to be the headlines and taglines buried all through the body copy if there's much copy at all. I hear it in the dialogue in the commercials.

A recent example—in the Ortho lawn commercials last summer, there was this great central selling idea that the smart wife would tell the dumb husband:

Our magic formula kills the weeds, not the grass!

What an amazing, specific proposition for anyone worried about their lawn. What a great potential Micro-Script, tagline, signature, anything.

I was positive I'd see that line at the bottom of the commercial. If this was Ted Bates, there wouldn't have been any question.

But instead, the onscreen tagline was:

Defend what's yours.

As usual (which is why my wife won't watch the news with me anymore), I jumped up from the couch screaming, "*What the hell kind of promise was that? They could've been selling burglar alarms, or exercise programs for skinny guys. I'm supposed to remember and repeat that to the Home Depot guy when I ask for the weed killer? 'I'm looking for a product to defend what's mine?'* I Wanna KILL SOME WEEEEEDS!"

Memo to big ad agency guys getting paid millions by Ortho: The headline's in the body copy.

Create Your Own

Another One...

The US Postal Service is doing a lot better in their advertising these days. I love the Micro-Script in the body of their current ads:

If it fits, it ships. (For one flat rate.)

I think it. I say it. It answers my questions without having to call!

Their tagline is *A simpler way to ship* which while not as nifty a little nugget as "If it fits, it ships," at least it states their overall company positioning and promise in a crystal clear, cogent way. Strategically, I know they need a broader, more comprehensive promise to cover much more than just shipping in their flat rate boxes. In these ads, *If it fits, it ships* is a Micro-Script that works as a great headline, paid off by a strong, descriptive tagline: *A simpler way to ship*. It's about "simple" and "shipping." Good. <u>Unlike</u> Defend what's yours.

But back to those little, less than a page stories you're going to write. In the case histories coming up, I'm going to show you what some actual stories look like.

4. Synthesize—Collect the Pieces and Put Together Micro-Scripts

If you've made a basic effort to jot down your story and include the best language and lines you've picked up thus far, then this is really the easiest part. Because now you just look at your story, and maybe an extraneous note or two and pull out the Micro-Script candidates that appear line by line in the narrative. They're just candidates of course until they prove themselves in the court of human repetition by someone other than you talking to your cat. Although a classic, *Meow Mix, cats ask for it by name!* probably came from conversation with a cat so don't count all cat conversations out.

You're looking for five or six stand-alone Micro-Scripts. Since they come out of the beginning, middle and end natural sequence of a story, you'll find they can also be easily snapped together to form a whole *Micro-Pitch*—our new word for "elevator speech"—no doubt the most powerful tool for any sales-oriented enterprise. Most organizations don't have a Micro-Pitch, even though they all know they should. Micro-Pitches will come in the next chapter.

Let's go to some real world cases now to illustrate how easy it is to peel the Micro-Scripts out of your narrative—the final part of mining your first set of scripts out of this process.

Real World Cases: Process in Action
Insurance that Rewards Responsible Homeowners

Narragansett Bay Insurance Company asked us to help find their Dominant Selling Idea, then turn it into Micro-Scripts and materials to activate a new brand position (DSI) in the marketplace.

1. We began our process at <u>Hypothesize</u>—sitting down and talking with as many Narragansett people as we could from the CEO down, then independent sales agents and experts in the industry.

The first questions were: so what's different about Narragansett? Why does the market need you? What do you offer that nobody else does?

We quickly found out a whole list of interesting facts and figures.

After a few giant hurricanes in the past decade—think Katrina—insurance companies that sold homeowners policies on the coasts were in a state of shock. The ones that weren't going bankrupt were fleeing the coastal business like evacuees, leaving it up to public agencies to provide government-supported coverage (complete with government-quality customer service).

Yet into this fray, swimming the other way, to save the day, came Narragansett Bay—a group of insurance entrepreneurs who saw a classic opportunity in what the industry calls a "dislocated market." Narragansett knew that if they applied advanced computer "CAT" (catastrophic) modeling, analyzing risks on a local grid vs. the regional, one-size-fits-all way of the old companies, they could turn the coastal market around. In other words, houses are different—one can be a completely different risk than the one next door, based on structure, orientation, and mostly, the responsible attitude of the owner. Narragansett just needed a way to tell good house from bad. And they found it—by combining advanced risk modeling with a decidedly low-tech, common sense technique: they actually went out in person and *looked at the houses.* Unlike the old companies, they did a visual safety appraisal of every new prospect's home. Most homes passed. But if your shingles were falling off they could ask you to fix them, or pass on the policy. As one agent told us—they were looking for *responsible homeowners* who already believed in protecting and maintaining their homes. When they found them, they could give them better insurance and include better features because they were better risks—they'd earned it. The change Narragansett Bay was able to bring to a distressed market by identifying "responsible homeowners" said it all.

2. During our conversations of course, we made sure to <u>Plagiarize</u>.

We heard lines from agents like: *They make insurance fit your home, they don't make your home fit their insurance.* Only Narragansett does this in-home, in-person appraisal because *insuring your home's too important to just do over the phone.* We heard *they give you more ways to customize—it's like wealthy home insurance for middle range homes.* We heard *homeowners insurance is all they do, so they know the most—and they'll still be here when all the other companies won't.* Finally, we heard that *responsible homeowners know they're different—they make fewer claims, they help hold down costs—so they should be treated differently* by their insurance company.

3. Next we <u>Memorialized</u> it in a brand story that could fit on one page or one PowerPoint slide. Here's the actual copy. I'll explain the underlines in a minute:

<u>Responsible homeowners are different</u>: they keep their <u>homes safer</u> and <u>make fewer insurance claims</u>. And since there's <u>something unique about every home</u>, they <u>don't want the usual one-size-fits-all homeowners insurance</u> that leaves you <u>underprotected</u> for loss, <u>or over-insured</u> with unnecessary premiums. They want the kind of <u>custom options, great service and savings</u> that <u>responsible homeowners deserve.</u>

Narragansett Bay agrees. That's why it's <u>the insurance company</u> specially <u>designed for responsible homeowners—people who</u> share its values of keeping homes safe and protected, who <u>prevent losses from happening in the first place</u>. Narragansett believes <u>these homeowners should be treated differently—rewarded with extra choices, service and benefits</u>.

It starts with their one-of-a-kind <u>programs like *ShelterPride*—</u> that includes an <u>in-home appraisal</u> for every new policyholder—because properly <u>insuring your home is too important to just do over the phone</u>. A Narragansett Bay representative <u>comes in-person, at no charge, to review your home's exposure</u> today, <u>show you better ways to avoid</u> loss tomorrow and <u>make sure you're getting every credit and discount you deserve</u>.

And <u>Narragansett Bay is *specialized*—homeowners insurance is all they do</u>—so they have more expert knowledge of risk factors in the localities they serve, and can <u>insure each home more individually</u>.

It means that Narragansett can indeed <u>offer more customized coverage and deductibles, more discounts and credits, faster, more personal claims service and the prospect of lower long-term rate increases</u> for their policyholders.

Simply said: <u>Narragansett Bay never forces your home to fit their insurance. They make their insurance fit your home. You've earned it</u> as a responsible homeowner—the kind who insures with Narragansett Bay.

Why are some phrases underlined?

They're the phrases and nuggets that judgment tells us will be the best Micro-Script material and we'll fashion them into

Micro-Scripts next. They went into making the story, providing color and context. Now we pull out a few of the best and re-constitute them, as...

4. Finally, We <u>Synthesized</u>.

And, then, we cull roughly six to seven Micro-Scripts of varying lengths out of the story that could either stand alone, or fit together in sequence to become a Micro-Pitch.

Here are the first seven:

1. **Narragansett's the insurance for responsible homeowners.**

2. **Responsible homeowners are different—they keep their homes safer and better—so they should be treated that way.**

3. **They believe the best loss is the one that never happens.**

4. **They give you more options, more credits, more discounts, without costing more.**

5. **They don't make your home fit the insurance, they make insurance fit your home.**

6. **Insuring your home's too important to just do by phone.**

7. **They're the only ones who visit every home. They go over your risk, double-check your coverage and make sure you get every credit you deserve.**

8. **Responsible homeowners get more with Narragansett Bay.**

Any person could use one, two or all these scripts to explain what sets Narragansett Bay Insurance apart to just about anyone.

> **Q**: Why aren't these as short and nifty as those two word Micro-Scripts like *Bridge to nowhere* or *domino theory?*
>
> **A**: Remember—Micro-Scripts can be as long as a few sentences or short as a word or two. Depends on the subject, the situation and the shorthand that develops over time. You can't get much shorter than *"Insurance for responsible homeowners"* shown above. And we're not at the tagline process yet which may yield other quickies. In fact, with taglines, we're always looking for that ultimate phrase that does the whole sale—a Micro-Pitch really, in a one single sentence. (see below).

The point is, you've gotten started—with a set of short, pithy phrases that convey a world of information.

Now you've got a fertilized egg…!

In the next chapter we'll show how easily these Micro-Scripts can be transformed into all the other core tools of messaging—like taglines, web copy, and your Micro-Pitch. But first…

An Even Quicker Case History
The World's First Car for People in Wheelchairs

It was the end of 2008 and the automobile business America-wide was on the verge of croaking like road kill on Route 66. Into this economy, a bunch of visionary investors decided to start a new car company. But, not just any kind of car company. VPG autos was going to build "purpose-driven" cars from the ground up—starting with the first car designed from scratch for people in wheelchairs.

Until then, the only cars a mobility-challenged person could buy were standard assembly line vans or SUVs—that then had to be chopped in half and rebuilt. You got a retro-fit, "conversion" vehicle that *cost twice as much but lasted half as long* as a regular car and *didn't even meet minimum crash test standards*.

The new company asked us to position and name the car. We conducted our HPMS process. We asked questions, we copied great language from people who'd been with the company since inception. We met people in wheelchairs and the people who care for them.

We got this story:

The First Car Built Especially
for People with Disabilities

For persons with disabilities, <u>buying a car has always been a costly compromise</u>. Your <u>only choice was to buy an "after-market" converted vehicle</u>—a factory van whose <u>frame was cut in half and its interior rebuilt by another shop to become accessible and ADA compliant</u>. This conversion process not only <u>doubles</u>

the cost, it leaves the frame weaker, heavier, less durable, worse riding and even voids the original factory warranties!

What if you could eliminate the compromises and design a better car—a "Mobility Vehicle" (MV) especially for persons with disabilities—while costing thousands less than a converted vehicle? We asked engineers, car owners, caregivers and advocates and here's what they told us...

First, there'd be no more *conversions*. You'd build it from the ground up for its purpose—not an aftermarket "afterthought" vehicle. That means you'd make it tough as a truck, but drive like a car. You'd design it with the help of the people who'll depend on it—so it would be more spacious, easier to maneuver inside, easier to carry cargo in the trunk, better to drive and simpler to enter and exit with wider doors and ramps. You'd make it more durable and reliable—with proven parts systems and a stronger body so it would last years longer, spend less time in the repair shop and cost less to maintain. This would make it safer too. In fact, it would keep its original factory warranties and safety ratings because its frame wouldn't be destroyed and rebuilt before its first mile.

You'd even change the *experience* of owning it. You'd pick up customers to come to the show room and pick the car up when it needed service.

Simply put—you'd take out the compromises.

That's why a new automotive company was formed to build this very vehicle—the first factory original vehicle especially for persons with disabilities. *The MV-1.* A vehicle that's improved in every way, yet costs less than most aftermarket MVs available today. The first car that's built from the ground up for people like us.

Now, here's the first set of Micro-Script candidates.

1. **If you're disabled, there's this special new car.**

2. **The first car for people in wheelchairs, *built from the ground up.***

3. <u>No</u> *more conversion* **means no more compromise—it's better in every way:**
   - Built tough as a truck, cause its frame's never cut.
   - But drives as easy as a regular car.
   - So roomy and safe, keeps all its warranties in place.
   - Yet *costs thousands less* than any conversion!

4. **Say goodbye to "aftermarket, afterthought."**

5. **Your time has come for the "MV-1."**

6. **The first real "Mobility Vehicle."**

7. **Built from the ground up for people like us.**

Re-prise, Re-vise

From here on in, the process is a matter of trying out your scripts in every different channel and venue—in sales conversations, in collateral material, in advertising, on your website, the blogs—and listening for what comes back. Some will be repeated outright. You'll know they've got the right stuff. Some come back with modifications by consumers and stakeholders in words or tenses. Use that feedback to adjust and edit. And some won't come back at all. Those you can discard unless they're useful in filler copy.

Make Listening a Core Strategy

In fact, make the logistics of listening a core strategy, taking Micro-Scripts in, making adjustments, and sending them back out to leverage two things—

1. *The genius of language that consumers will offer back—and*

2. *The engine of trust, that consumers will now control.*

We must use all the new media tools to set up a perpetual feedback loop—the links, the social network connections, and all the other online mechanics that make it easier to talk. Think of it as your *Micro-Script power grid.*

Then let consumers and champions hand you Micro-Script gold. Airborne cold supplements, the famous over-the-counter product that was *invented by a second grade teacher* and one of my favorite Word-of-Mouth-generated success stories, got one of it's greatest Micro-Scripts from customers who told them *you take it before you get on a plane to keep from getting a cold.* That went into their advertising and their packaging and contributed greatly to their legend. The company wasn't even thinking of an air travel connection when they named the product. They called it Airborne because of all the airborne germs in second grade classrooms. It was their frenzied fans who jumped to the conclusion that the name Airborne must have something to do with planes, too, and quickly generated the take it before you get on the airplane torture test Micro-Script. The company just listened.

It Worked for Me with "Micro-Scripts" Itself

When I first started thinking about Micro-Scripts, I was looking for a memorable term to express it. "Micro-Scripts" turned out to be the term that when I'd say it, people would say it back almost immediately whenever I got in a discussion. If I put the term in a speech, I heard speakers who followed me use the term. Audience members used it in their questions. That's how I knew *my* Micro-Script candidate was indeed a Micro-Script for real.

And as I talked about it with people, new language and phrases came up that others were especially prone to repeat. How did I know? People would casually recycle these phrases in conversation—like they were already familiar.

Phrases like *Five words are more powerful than 5,000* and *It's not what they hear, it's what they repeat, Tell a story in a sentence* and *Every screen's a Word of Mouth Machine* made the team as walk-ons this way. "Five words are more powerful" was a phrase I plagiarized from someone else describing Micro-Scripts. I started using it and people kept repeating it. There it was. A Micro-Script.

The Marketing Gift that Keeps on Giving

From here, from the 150 words or so and the six or seven phrases you've got in your first set of Micro-Scripts, you've got the foundation for an entire go-to-market communications program. You can assemble a tagline, names in some cases, brochure and website content, key PR phrases—and that all-important Micro-Pitch that you can tell to anyone, even if your ride only lasts for one floor.

The important thing is, by using your Micro-Script foundation, your communications and your champions' communications will *automatically* be sharper, quicker, more consistent and more on brand strategy than ever before. Micro-Scripts are the great focuser and aligner—maybe their biggest advantage of all.

In the next chapter, we'll show how easy it is to make Micro-Pitches, Micro-Mission Statements, taglines and other core communications out of your Micro-Scripts.

Remember the Rules for The Creative Process

1. <u>Hypothesize</u>—Ask a lot of questions, even if you think you know the answers.

2. <u>Plagiarize</u>—Borrow the best language and practices of the superstars on your sales force or in your field.

3. <u>Memorialize</u>—write out a simple, short story—"The headline's always in the copy."

4. <u>Synthesize</u>—Peel off the initial Micro-Scripts, combine with other nuggets you've collected.

Then, Reprise and Revise!

CHAPTER 8

Micro-Messaging

Micro-Pitches, Mission Statements, Taglines, Twitter and more...

Micro-Messaging: Every Key Communication Needs to Go Micro

It doesn't get simpler than that. If it's a core piece of communications material, an elevator speech, a corporate mission statement, a PR key point—it needs to be able to work in Micro form if you want to make it work—that is, get share of screen in today's Word of Mouth world. That means its goal is to do its job in as short a phrase as possible, and it needs to use Micro-Script techniques to make it say-able and play-able. Call it *Micro-Messaging.*

Start With Your Micro-Pitch

Everybody in business knows the advantage of having a crisp, compelling elevator speech. Few in business have one— one that actually would work in the few seconds of an elevator ride, causing a prospect to say to you, "Gee, can you call me?

Here's my card." Or one that anybody agrees on and can actually recite. Most of the time, you ask twenty people in a company what the elevator pitch is and you'll get ten different stories and ten blank stares. Think of all the wasted sales opportunities for millions of organizations.

We've renamed this all-important selling tool the **Micro-Pitch** for a few good reasons:

- It's automatically generated by connecting your Micro-Scripts.
- It forces you to keep it short, sharp and focused.
- It has Micro-Script DNA so it's even more memorable.
- You don't have a whole elevator ride to expound any-more. Your Micro-Pitch has to be able to work in a single floor!

The wonderful fact is, once you've pulled six or seven Micro-Script candidates out of your brand story, your Micro-Pitch is done. All you have to do is add a few connection words and *voila!*

I'll go back to the VPG Autos scripts from the previous chapter to show you.

Here are the initial scripts:

1. **If you're disabled, there's this special new car.**

2. **The first car for people in wheelchairs, *built from the ground up.***

3. <u>No</u> *more conversion* means no more compromise—it's better in every way:
   - Built tough as a truck, cause its frame's never cut.
   - But drives as easy as a regular car.
   - So roomy and safe, keeps all its warranties in place.
   - Yet *costs thousands less* than any conversion!

4. Say goodbye to "aftermarket, afterthought."

5. Your time has come for the "MV-1."

6. The world's first "Mobility Vehicle."

7. Built from the ground up for people like us.

Now you just string 'em together, backward or forward, into a Micro-Pitch. You don't have to use every word, just enough to tell the story—

83-Word Micro-Pitch for the MV-1

If you're disabled, there's this special new car—
The first car for people in wheelchairs, built from the ground up.
(So there's) <u>no more conversions</u>, *no more compromises—*
   - *It's tough as a truck, cause its frame's never cut.*
   - *But it drives as easy as a regular car.*
   - *It's so roomy and safe, it keeps its warranties in place.*
   - *Yet it costs thousands less than any conversion vehicle!*
So say goodbye to "aftermarket, afterthought."

The time has come for the "MV-1."

Look how easy it is to get a Micro-Pitch out of it. After all, it's already written. You just add the connecting words here and there between phrases if you need them.

The one above takes about thirty seconds to say. Because it's so modular, you can subtract some of the scripts if you don't have time. Or stick new and better ones in if you find something better.

The One Sentence Micro-Pitch: Going All the Way!

Okay, let's put our money where our mouth is.

Ultimately—as we've said all along, a Micro-Pitch can be as short as a single sentence. After all, Splenda did it with *Made from sugar so it tastes like sugar.*

That's enough to sell me in seven words.

Or *The milk chocolate that melts in your mouth, not in your hand.*

And here's an all-time favorite of mine in a name: *The Oreck 8-lb. Hotel Vac.* A six word name/tagline-in-one tells me in specific terms that it's incredibly light, incredibly durable because it undergoes the hotel torture test, and incredibly effective for the same reasons.

Those were all superb taglines that doubled as Micro-Pitches in and of themselves. Imagine doing an entire presentation just by saying one sentence. Or, as we saw in Chapter 6, an entire memoir in six words.

So can it always be done?

No.

Some products or companies are just too complex to summarize in one line. But is it the ultimate achievement when you can? Yes it is. The one-sentence Micro-Pitch. To get down to that level with your company, to let it all ride on a sentence, to do it for the MV-1 for example, you'd need a little trial and error to prove you were completing your sale. But the effort is invariably worth it.

For the MV-1, I'd volunteer a line like:

The first car that's built from the ground up, for people like us.

And now here's a Micro-Pitch you could make from the Narragansett Bay Insurance scripts in the previous chapter:

The Narragansett Bay Micro-Pitch

Narragansett Bay does more for responsible homeowners. Because when it comes to protecting your home—they know you do more, so you should get more—without paying more.

They give you more options, more credits, more service—but not more premiums.

(For instance), they're the only company that does an in-person appraisal of every home—to double-check your coverage, and make sure you get every credit you deserve.

They don't make your home fit the insurance, they make the insurance fit your home. (And that's why) for responsible homeowners, your #1 choice is
…Narragansett Bay.

I think anybody from a receptionist to a CEO could handle a story like that.

And if I wanted to compress it into a single line, I might bring it down to:

Where responsible owners insure they get more. Or...

'Responsible' pays at Narragansett Bay. Or...

The #1 choice for responsible homeowners.

All the above are close. But you wouldn't know which of these was the absolute winner, the catchiest repeater, until you tested it, or at least tried it out on people and let them pick the winner. In Micro-Scripts, *the customer is always right.*

Which now takes us to the subject of taglines. The one liner Micro-Pitches above could easily double as really powerful taglines. And in real life, they do.

Using Your Micro-Scripts to Create Powerful, Repeatable Taglines...

As we said earlier, a tagline written in Micro-Script is *always* a better tagline and should always be your objective in any tagline exercise. Why? Because it tells an interesting story about your product, or a key piece of one. It's a story bite. That makes it set you apart and inform and sell, every time you see it or say it.

Here's one of my favorites:

Kashi is 7 whole grains on a mission.

What an amazing, unique parcel of information is contained in those eight words.

And FedEx created a whole new category and still owns it to this day, with its original line: *When it absolutely, positively has to be there overnight.* What more did I need to know? And nobody ever forgot *Wheaties, breakfast of champions.* Not for over eighty years, that is.

Compare those to *A passion to make a difference.* Or *Now you're eating.* The kind of thing you see that's written by advertisers who don't understand that these could apply to any of 100 different products, they're dismissed as empty claims, they inspire nothing and give me no reason to waste my breath and my listener's time by repeating. There's nothing in it for either party. They're invisible.

If I actually wanted to tell a friend about one of these invisibly-tagged companies, I'd make up my own Micro-Scripts to impart some worthwhile information. I'd never think of using their taglines.

Again, going through the HPMS exercise and coming up with a starting list of Micro-Scripts almost assures you that you'll create meatier, meaningful taglines if you stick to your knitting when tagline time comes. Micro-Scripts will serve to guide and focus you as usual.

So what one-liners could we come up with out of the MV-1 Mobility Vehicle Micro-Scripts?

I'll offer a few:

The New MV-1:

> **The first car that's built from the ground up, for people like us.**

No more conversion means no more compromise.

Tough as a truck, cause its frame's never cut.

Works like a truck, drives like a car.

MV-1. Compromise Done.

Your first real "Mobility Vehicle."

The first car designed with wheelchairs in mind.

A passion for excellence. (Just kidding.)

Mission Statements in Micro

Companies seem to love to write mission statements. Employees love to ignore them. Corporations don't love to spend millions on consultants to write them, just to have employees ignore them, but that's what happens to them.

Why?

Because too many Fortune 500 companies write them like this:

> *Guided by relentless focus on our five imperatives, we will constantly strive to implement the critical initiatives required to achieve our vision. In doing this, we will deliver operational excellence in every corner of the company and meet or exceed our commitments to the many constituencies we serve. All of our long-term strategies and short-term actions will be molded*

by a set of core values that are shared by each and every associate.

Guess what business they're in?

And another Fortune 500 company probably spent a year to write this:

We are a market-focused, process-centered organization that develops and delivers innovative solutions to our customers, consistently outperforms our peers, produces predictable earnings for our shareholders, and provides a dynamic and challenging environment for our employees.

Guess what business they're in?

Does it matter? The first is a famous supermarket chain. The second is a big oil company.

Mission statements are supposed to be created to give employees a rallying cry, a place to focus, an inspirational driver. But even if I tried to memorize those above, I'd forget in five minutes. And I wouldn't understand them anyway. Is it any wonder why employees look clueless when you ask them, "are you guided by your mission statement?"

By this point in our book, the solution shouldn't be that hard to figure. We know what the answer is. If you want people who are bombarded by messaging daily to internalize yours, then follow the new rules: write them in Micro-Script.

Like the following example:

It was inspired by a TV infomercial I saw last week that showed me how it's done.

The CEO came on TV for a product called BackJoy. Not a bad TV product name for a shaped seat orthotic (ass-thotic) you put in a chair to help you sit better and relieve back stress for people who are immobile in cubicles all day.

The CEO said: "I'm going to tell you our mission statement in nine words:

We're going to fix the way the world sits."

I thought—you just reminded me to tell the readers that we need to fix the way the world writes core communications like mission statements by using Micro-Scripts that employees can actually use as a daily mantra.

Here's another one. Frank Kelleher, the CEO of legendary brand Southwest Airlines said back in the airline's early days: "Every employee knows exactly how to run our airline and how to make the right decisions. All they have to do is remember our mission statement:

We're the low cost airline."

So I say unto you—

If you believe enough in your mission statement or any statement to want others to hear it, follow it; if you want it to guide, inspire and inform, make it one that people can remember and repeat. Make it short, swift, singular and sage. Use the power of Micro-Scripts.

The maker of the MV-1 car for people in wheelchairs could say the mission statement like this:

We're going to manufacture the world's best, most accessible Mobility Vehicles—economically, mechanically and functionally— from the ground up.

Twitter Too

By now we should all be attuned to a very important reality. It goes for all expressions in all media—old, new and social:

Just because it's <u>short</u>, doesn't make your message a Micro-Script. The word count doesn't make it memorable, impactful, penetrating, effective or smart.

For that, a message needs to contain Micro-Script elements—story pieces, colorful language, and provocative construction if you care that it be anything but noise.

A Tweet like this is not a Micro-Script:

Say LOL at bit.ly/85gq5W/m5tyq.

You might as well be speaking in Microsoft DOS.

To be fair, I know the vast majority of these kinds of messages are not *intended* to be great oratory. They're nothing more than alerts and idle chatter for your friends.

But there are indeed thousands if not millions of folks who *are* attempting to broadcast meaningful, penetrating communications—about news events, professional issues, opportunities, lives and careers.

And to all of you I say—apply the Micro-Script rules if you want your Tweets to be something more than worldwide static; if you want them to be noticed, absorbed, internalized and influential to the max.

If memoirs can be written in six words, then you can write me a Tweet with an <u>idea</u> in it. And people will thank you.

Same for Google

While at a marketing conference in India, a very savvy Internet CEO told me that research shows *"over 50% of the Google subject lines—those blue headers that appear on the results page—actually <u>dissuade</u> readers, rather than persuade them to stop and click."*

I haven't been able to independently check this assertion. But a little thumbnail polling of my colleagues and my own experience tells me the statement's true. Every Google header is a headline, competing for a click on a page with ten competing appeals. Stands to reason that if you took a Micro-Script/Micro-Pitch approach to the construction of these instant pick-up lines, your stop and click percentage would go way up.

Look at any Google results page. How many of the headers are confusing, vague, frustratingly opaque? But when I happen upon a clear one—a discernible idea, an actual compelling promise—I grab for it. It's a breath of fresh air. It gets my click.

And according to my webmaster friends, these header lines no longer need to be a randomly generated Google thing. You can control those headers. And that means, you should, you must—as much as you'd control any advertising message you'd want the world to see. And since at this moment my IT lady's not answering her phone, you're going to have to ask *your* webmaster friends exactly how to go into Google and write yours.

As you might surmise, I'm preaching here and I hope by now you're the choir. We agree that the social media and Internet portals are game changers of historic proportions.

But *what* you say is still at least as important as how you leverage new media to say it. Random words and gimmicks may amuse and distract, but only **an idea** of differentiating value can put people in motion. And that takes us to the final chapter...

Remember the Rules for Communicating Everything

1. *Your Micro-Scripts are the gift that keep on giving*—use them at the core of all your communication.

2. *Make Micro-Messaging Your Default*—for sales pitches, mission statements, taglines, websites, social media posting—anything you want to say that's worth remembering.

CHAPTER 9

Survival of the Simplest

Call it an obsession but once you start thinking about the heuristic-loving human brain, how it thrives on simplicity and speed; once you grasp this as essential truth going forward into the new media age, you start seeing Micro-Script traces everywhere you look.

I just found out that the God of the Hebrews, YHWH him/herself used them in the original Ten Commandments, so that even the most illiterate, dust-ridden slaves could memorize them on the fingers of both hands during the Exodus. All ten had to be available on demand since he/she hadn't brought forth text messaging yet.

Thomas Cahill, the literary and biblical scholar in *The Gifts of the Jews* explained that what we call The Ten "Commandments" was written so tersely—to be memorable and repeatable—that in the original Hebrew they were called the Ten *Words*. "Thou shalt not steal" simply appeared as *"no-steal."* The Ten Words came out as: *no-kill, no-adulter, no-lie,* and so on.

So I guess you don't have to take my word for it after all, because even *God used Micro-Scripts!*

A Few Concluding Thoughts and Themes

I'd planned to continue our discussion for another 500 or 600 pages, until I realized that it might get awkward for a book about "five words being more powerful than 5,000" to go on for too long.

So here are a few big themes I hope you'll take with you from here on…

The title of this chapter says it all really. As the world of everything gets more complex, **simplicity** and those who know how to make it so will be the ones who win in any almost any arena. They will be followed, they will be formidable, they will be heard and harkened to. They will provide ever-greater relief to the minions mired in the merde.

Their products, their companies, their words and solutions will be sought after, not because they superficialize, but because they prioritize.

They, the Simplifiers, will be the ones that get us to truth—guided by one of the most essential truths: *to be successful and happy, we must learn to* ***focus on a much smaller set of much more important things.*** And not just the material things. It's every bit as critical for ideas, words and relationships.

Micro-Scripts will be one of the Simplifier's primary tools.

Also, please remember:

Micro-Scripts both Giveth and Taketh Away...
Tactics and Counter-Tactics

Any powerful tool can be used for negative purposes unless those of us on the good side counter with positive. The more Yin, the more Yang—it's a universal law. Take the Internet. Look at all the good it's bringing us. All the knowledge, all the democracy, all the empowering of people that never could have had a voice. Now look at all the scary bad it threatens us with. It's enabled terrorists to crawl out of their caves in places like Waziristan and threaten us globally. It publishes the formulas for fertilizer bombs. It's obliterating privacy and security. Albert Einstein—who some believe had his own private line to the almighty—said his great fear was that "our technology would exceed our humanity." Let's hope the Internet ultimately is a net force for good because it sure isn't going away.

Micro-Scripts work in the same way. How should we react when they're being used against us?

The ancient Micro-Script, *fight fire with fire* applies here. When faced with scurrilous scripts, the only tactic is to provide fresh and powerful Micro-Scripts of one's own, not hide and accuse the other side of foul play.

The cardinal rule is—you're reinforcing your opponent's message when you make whiney denials of "No it's not." "They're not telling you the truth." "They're distorting the facts!"

Instead, you must: 1) turn their own actual scripts against them by word and name, and 2) reframe the whole debate with provocative, vivid, memorable counter-scripts.

They labeled John Kerry *the flip-flopper* in the 2004 Presidential election because he had indeed changed his mind on some issues, then provided the Bush team with great dumb quotes like *I was for it before I was against it.* But Kerry used the wrong counter-tactics—hoping it would go away by whining, "No I'm not."

If they had tossed the hand grenade right back at Bush who had "flip-flopped" just as glaringly as Kerry—if they had opened fire with Micro-Scripts of their own—they could have extinguished "flip-flopper" in a week. Instead, Kerry invited a Micro-Script disaster.

You can't fight a Micro-Script with a manifesto. In the heat of a political or marketing battle, a Micro-Script is a bullet. A manifesto is a blur.

Be a Crusader for Content...

Not the cheap, throw-away commodity kind of "content" that's blithely defined by new-media pundits. I mean the original kind. Substance.

Our parents, teachers and even our kiddie TV shows used to remind us everyday that: *It's what's inside that counts. Beauty is only skin deep. You can't judge a book by its cover.* And if you were watching PBS: *Form follows function.*

Content was about the idea, the character, the asset underlying the bubble. They understood that the medium can have great significance—no doubt, TV and the Internet have changed the world. But the medium can never replace the message. The medium doesn't figure out $E=MC^2$, the cure for AIDS or the lines in *Hamlet*. Those aren't the pipeline, they're the whole point.

As for the savants out there saying outrageous things like "strategy is dead," or relegating content to anonymous filler like the air that fills a balloon, my belief is that they either hope to profit from selling the media, or they don't understand the difference between the air and the balloon.

They're offering you a Tupperware party without the Tupperware. Medium without the message.

Micro-Scripts give you the *intel inside* of this media maelstrom—ideas and substance incarnate, so you can communicate and above all, *differentiate* with unique impact in a saturated, superficial world.

Remember that Micro-Messaging is for Everyone...

If by chance you are a lawyer delivering a closing argument that you want the jury to take back to the jury room, then I'd advise you to remember: *If the glove doesn't fit, you must acquit*, the absence of either gloves or Kato Kaelin in your case notwithstanding.

And I had a doctor friend tell me that it's no different when you're instructing interns who have been up 24 hours straight, trying to get them to absorb the bottom line in a teaching situation. Here's one he'd remind students of when it came to strokes: *Time loss is brain loss*. He said the best medical professors were always trying to come up with ones like that.

Because The Brain Always Gets Its Way...

Today, it's the only way. The more stress and chaos, the more our brains switch to auto-pilot. They think less and less about what they are going to think about. They rely on heuristic rules of thumb more than ever. They love what they understand and they love the person who helps them understand it. They love it fast, short and simple. They love it in story form. They love the heart of the matter when you show it to them. They love truth and value. They love a success and survival advantage.

These are our instincts. Our chemistry. No technology or media advance will *ever* change it one iota.

And that's why we apply the Micro-Script Rules.

For the Last Time...

Why would anyone jump out of a perfectly good airplane?

In the final, final analysis, for anyone with a business, a story to tell or a point to make, what this is all about is the <u>magic of focus</u>. Focus gives you the power, persistence and creativity you never thought you had to concentrate on the heart of the matter. And that's critical to every area of decision making in life—not just marketing.

How do you focus, if you're focus-challenged like most of us in this world? To focus, the main thing you need to do is ... *commit.*

I don't recommend the following method to everyone, but I'll tell you how I found out this little secret:

I became a skydiver because I couldn't hit a golf ball straight. Nowadays, when you skydive the first time, you do what's called a tandem jump where you're actually strapped onto the instructor. Your tandem lesson is an all of five-minute course. The instructor tells you that when you're up at 14,000 feet and standing at the door—he's going to shout you one final question:

Survival of the Simplest

ARE YOU READY TO SKYDIVE—because it has to be your own free will and testament. But with all the noise and commotion, he suggests that *no* often sounds just like *go* and *I don't wanna go* sounds like *Geronimo!* What he's telling you is, once the plane's off the ground, you're pretty much going to do this. You stand in that door. You take one little step. And just like that…there's a million-mile gulf between the metal threshold where you just were, and the place out in space where you suddenly are. You're committed. Boy, are you committed. But the most amazing thing happens. You are more focused than you've ever been in your life on one big idea. Not sweating the small stuff, believe me. Everything's clear.

Committing to that one big thing and clearing away all those tempting secondary things in any critical endeavor can be almost as hard as jumping out of a perfectly good airplane. It takes guts to commit. <u>In fact—fear of making that one choice is the main reason *Why Johnny Can't Brand*.</u> But when you do, it's liberating. It unleashes creativity. Confidence. It energizes you and your people. And the job gets done.

In all of human communication, Micro-Scripts commit you, empower you and focus you as surely as that little step you take from the door to infinity in your first skydive. When it comes to focus, Micro-Scripts are as guaranteed as gravity.

Find your Micro-Scripts. Build them on your Dominant Selling Idea. And you'll have a new power to change your world.

163

About the Author

Bill Schley is an award-winning marketer, author and international speaker on communications. He is President of David ID, the branding firm known for creating the Dominant Selling Idea at some of the world's largest companies. His book *Why Johnny Can't Brand* was honored as a "Top 5 Marketing Book of the Year" by *Strategy+Business Magazine*. He  is an Alumnus of the legendary Ted Bates advertising agency, Harvard University, a trans-Atlantic sailor and avid skydiver.

Email Bill at: bill@billschley.com
bschley@davidid.com

Visit us and share your own Micro-Scripts at:
www.Micro-Scripts.com

Acknowledgments

I'm not just saying this to be nice. They are saints: every teacher who had me for English and didn't give up and move to Fiji. Starting with Mr. Y and Ms. Garabedian, and later but not least, Mr. Charlie Thomas and Mr. Roger F. Duncan, the Captain, who taught me about compound sentences. And later still, when it got to selling something, the *real* "Brand Titan" Bob Froelich, and Mark Schwatka at Ted Bates on 1515 Broadway, who tried to teach me how to make stories fit in 70 words and how to write an execution. From here we go all the way to Len Schley, author of the Granite Pages, whose natural Micro-Scripting brain came up with classic after classic when we were kids, without even realizing it—but we did. His talent for cutting to the heart of any matter in pico seconds is unexceeded to this day. His talent for driving Harriet crazy didn't keep her from calmly, patiently proofing and improving every paper or birthday poem I ever wrote. Also Chico "Mike" Chvany who at first could only sing but later became…instrumental, and collaborated through the most formative creative adventures. Next there are the people who were instrumental in bringing *The Micro-Script Rules* to fruition. Mark Walsh for inviting me onto his radio show and seeding the conversation that made the light bulb go off—a Micro-Script legend himself. There is the unfailing encouragement of Donna Volpitta, Ed.D who had wonderful ideas and smart suggestions from start to finish, giving of her time pro bono, way beyond the call of duty; and Nettie Hartsock, journalist, editor, new media maven and wise person par excellence. I thank Carl Nichols Jr., my partner at David ID, for his steadfast challenges to clarify and simplify. Finally there are Martha, Daniel and Sara, always supporting; Emily and Brooke who said they liked it, and Alec—who was a great help in editing the earliest versions. And Annie, to whom the book is dedicated, fairy princess that picked the one frog to kiss who…well, remained one—and thereby had to put up daily with every escapade, self-indulgent mood and literary project, for lo these many years.

Honestly—you should buy this book, at full cover price, for her sake.

WLS

Endnotes

1. *Gut Feelings, The Intelligence of the Unconscious* by Gerd Gigerenzer; Penguin Group USA, 2007 p. 11
2. Quotation by Steven Quartz in Op Ed Article by David Brooks, *New York Times;* April 7, 2009
3. *Gut Feelings, The Intelligence of the Unconscious* by Gerd Gigerenzer; Penguin Group USA, 2007 p. 16
4. Ibid., p. 174
5. Ibid., p. 18
6. *Unlimited Selling Power;* Donald Moine and Kenneth Lloyd; Prentice Hall, 1990 p. 174
7. *Why Johnny Can't Brand: Rediscovering the Lost Art of the Big Idea;* Bill Schley, Carl Nichols, Jr.; Penguin Group USA, 2005 p. 186
8. From the song *Lobachevsky* by Tom Lehrer

Index

Index

Index

"raw material" for micro-scripts, 113–119
repetition
    Dominant Selling Ideas and, 80
    effective micro-scripts and, 13–14, 17–18, 21, 26–29, 32, 45, 48, 51, 56, 65, 85–86, 109, 127, 130
repetitive word patterns, micro-scripts and, 96–97
"reprising," effective micro-scripts and, 113, 139. *See also* repetition.
"revising," in creative process, 113, 139
rhyme, micro-scripts and, 92, 96–97, 102
rhythm, micro-scripts and, 31, 45, 92, 96–98, 102
rules of thumb. *See* heuristics.

sales, micro-scripts and, 54–62, 103–105, 143–148
sales pitches. *See* micro-pitches.
scripts, sales, 59–60, 120, 124
Simon, Herbert A., 8
simplicity
    Dominant Selling Ideas and, 78–79
    heuristics and, 5, 8–9, 12, 24, 47
    increasing importance of, 158
    See also "big idea," having just one.
Simpson, O.J., 5

"six honest serving men," 115
slogans, micro-scripts and, 29
Smith Magazine, 93
social media, micro-scripts for, 153–154
sound bites, micro-scripts vs., 19–20, 29–30
Southwest Airlines micro-script, 152
specificity, Dominant Selling Ideas and, 79–80, 111
Splenda
    Dominant Selling Idea for, 71–72
    micro-pitch for, 146
    micro-scripts and, 48–49, 146
Starbucks, performance of, 75
"Stark Reminder" (template), 91–92
stories
    creating micro-scripts and, 125–130, 132–134
    effective micro-scripts and, 92–96, 148
    metaphor and, 31, 127
    sales communications and, 55
story bites, micro-scripts and, 19–20, 28, 54, 92, 125–128, 148
story pieces, micro-scripts and, 28, 53
substance, micro-scripts and, 160–161
"synthesizing," in creative process, 129–130, 134

CPSIA information can be obtained at www.ICGtesting.com
Printed in the USA
244490LV00002B/7/P